The Well-Lived Life

The Well-Lived Life

Live with Purpose
and Be Remembered

LYNDSAY GREEN

PATRICK CREAN EDITIONS
HarperCollins*PublishersLtd*

Published by Patrick Crean Editions,
an imprint of HarperCollins Publishers Ltd

First edition

HarperCollins books may be purchased for educational, business,
or sales promotional use through our Special Markets Department.

HarperCollins Publishers Ltd
Bay Adelaide Centre, East Tower
22 Adelaide Street West, 41st Floor
Toronto, Ontario, Canada
M5H 4E3

www.harpercollins.ca

Library and Archives Canada Cataloguing in Publication
information is available upon request.

ISBN 978-1-4434-5576-3

Printed and bound in the United States

LSC/C 9 8 7 6 5 4 3 2 1

For Cole and Charlie

Contents

Introduction

I began to think about legacy when my best friend was killed in a car crash. She was fifty years old and left behind two teenage sons. Her dog also died in the accident. This was fortunate, since he would have died of a broken heart anyway. My friend and I met when we were eighteen and called one another KS, for "kindred spirit." For much of our friendship, we lived in different cities and were so psychically connected we would spontaneously phone one another at the exact same time and get a busy signal. On the day she died, I was watching a play, blissfully unaware. At some point in the first act, I began to sob uncontrollably. My husband was alarmed, since the play was a comedy. When he asked why I was crying, I replied, "I don't know. I'm just terribly, terribly sad." While I was weeping, my friend's ex-husband and boyfriend were both leaving messages on my home phone asking me to call them urgently.

What is KS's legacy? Through the days of grief that followed her death, there was a thin silver lining. The outpouring of outrage over the accident, and the caring and concern for her family, meant that her photo was reproduced everywhere.

And it was a gorgeous professional photograph she had just commissioned. She would have been thrilled with the timing of the photo shoot. And she would have been in profound sorrow and utter disbelief to find that her life had been wrenched away from her. We were both descended from long-living matrilineal lines and were convinced we would be celebrating our one-hundredth birthdays together. From our perspective, she had been robbed of half her life. Knowing her certainty about her longevity, I assumed that she would have been completely unprepared for this tragic end and that she would have given little thought to her legacy. But, as I was to discover, my assumption was wrong.

KS's death happened almost two decades ago and I have stayed close to her family, especially her elder son. Our relationship is one of her legacies, as is the strong hold she still has on my heart. But one thing bothers me to this day: I never asked KS how she saw her legacy. After her death, her work colleagues stepped up to organize a lecture series in her name at the local university. Her career had been groundbreaking, and in many ways, this focus on her professional contribution made sense. So, I set up a fundraising campaign to support the project. But my heart wasn't in it. I knew she was so much more than her work, this woman of many passions. I felt I could have swayed the outcome if I'd been able to say, "We talked about this and she said she would like to be remembered with ... " But that conversation never happened.

What alarms people about this story is the abruptness of the end. We assume we'll have time to think through our legacy:

time to compose a meaning to our lives, time to follow a path closer to our life's purpose, time to make amends, time to clean up our mess. But a death like KS's reminds us our lives may be cut short at any time, and the call "Time's up!" may be sounded before we've paid attention to the implications of our end.

Looking back on KS's death, I wanted to learn more about her legacy. What has been her impact these many years later? Her professional accomplishments are easy to spot, but what about the influence she had on her family, friends and community? She left behind dependants and loved ones, including two teenage sons, a boyfriend who was living in the house she owned, her ex-husband, an elderly mother and an extended family. How did she plan for their needs? She had a full and rich life. What did she count as her seminal accomplishments? Did she record her story for her descendants? Did she have any regrets?

I was asking these questions because I was thinking about my own legacy. How would I feel if I knew my life was to end abruptly? Had I been living a life aligned with my values? Would my time on earth have made a difference to anyone or anything? What would I be leaving behind for those I loved? What responsibilities would be left dangling? What story would people tell about me after I was gone? Had I been taking full advantage of this one precious life, both for myself and for others?

I was curious about what other people were doing about their legacies. Were they deciding to change paths while they still could and, if so, what was motivating them to reorient themselves? Were they planning to right wrongs or fix problems, and how? I wondered whether people were recording their existence to leave some permanent traces for history. And what about those aspects of our legacy that require legal documents and financial commitments? How were people deciding what to put in their wills? Were they leaving a legacy donation, and how were they figuring out what organizations to support? How were they choosing the executor of their estate? Were they going to try and control from the grave, and did that make sense?

I discovered there's not much guidance for legacy planning. We know about the larger-than-life characters who win international awards, save species, or have buildings named after themselves. Their legacies seem guaranteed. But what about the rest of us who hope to live a good life, to make a small difference, to be remembered fondly by family and friends, and to make amends for our omissions or commissions before we're gone?

When I told people I was writing a book on legacy, I occasionally met with defensiveness. Some assumed I was focusing on material wealth and said the topic wouldn't apply to them because they wouldn't be leaving behind an inheritance and would be lucky if they had enough money to meet their own needs. Others said they had accomplished nothing of note and would not be remembered. Others said it was vanity and hubris to pursue a legacy. Some said they didn't want to think about their legacy, either because they were too young to think about death or because they couldn't bear to face their own mortality.

This book responds to these perspectives and emphasizes the reality that we are all leaving a legacy—for better or worse—and it warrants our attention. Whether consciously or not, we are building our legacy continuously and shaping it by the way we lead our lives. The actions we take and the contributions we make every day are the components that will structure our remembered self. As well, our future persona will be coloured by the attention we pay to the impact of our deaths on those we leave behind and our efforts to fill the gap left by our departure. In this regard, we would be wise not to underestimate the importance of the role we play on this earth. We may not have family responsibilities, but we may have a pet, and who would care for our animal if we weren't there? Maybe we're providing a service to our neighbour or our community, and who would take over that duty? And when it comes to material legacy, all of us will leave something, and the amount of attention that should be paid to our legacies is unrelated to the size of our estates. Our material bequests could include the literal giving of ourselves through donating organs. The letter we leave with our effects or the small memento we gift may have more meaning for the recipients than money. And, as the life of my friend KS illustrates, we're never too young to think about our legacy, because death could arrive at any moment.

The stories you'll read in this book have convinced me that approaching our lives with an eye to improving our afterlife can also deepen our present. By facing and accepting our mortality, we can enhance our lives in the here and now and leave a more profound imprint after we're gone. When we confront our legacy, we have to admit that our lives matter— not just now but after we're gone, and they matter not just to us but to others. In the next section, I look at how I gathered my stories for this book and how they turned my understanding of legacy into a kaleidoscope of meaning.

Background

Once I began to think about legacy, I encountered the concept at every turn. Obituaries praised the *legacy* of the deceased, describing their impact on others and how they would be remembered. Broadcasters talked about the *legacy* of record-breaking athletes. Analysts predicted the *legacy* of political and legal decisions. A *New Yorker* cartoon showed parents holding up their newborn baby with the caption, "We're already wondering what her *legacy* might be."[1] There were media interviews with people struggling with the negative *legacy* of family, societal or governmental abuse. And there were discussions about positive *legacy* from moral teachings or exemplary behaviour handed down by families and cultures.

While these references to non-material *legacy* were everywhere, just as common were the uses of the term in its material sense, meaning a bequest. Glancing through theatre programs, charity annual reports or hospital newsletters, I would find a list of "*legacy* donors"—those individuals who had promised to leave financial donations to the organization in their wills. I learned about Leave a Legacy, an educational program of the

Canadian Association of Gift Planners, which encourages people to leave gifts for their favourite charity or non-profit organization in their wills. And when people spoke to me about
wills, they mentioned the *legacy* gifts they wanted to leave to
others, as well as those they had received themselves.

I began to accept that this ubiquitous use of the word *legacy*
was not merely sloppy use of language but rather an accurate
reflection of the composite nature of who we will be in the
world after our death. We are in the constant process of legacy
formation, shaped by the lives we are living, melded with the
concrete things we are giving now or planning to leave behind
to our family, our community and the world. Our legacies will
comprise both these abstract and concrete elements melded
from material and non-material components to form our
afterlife. It is in this context you will find me using the terms
"afterlife" and "life after death" to refer to the ways in which
we will continue to exist in the memories of those whose
lives we have touched, and through the lasting impact of our
actions. This is how we are creating our symbolic immortality,
day by day.

So, this book is about legacy writ large, and I have been
as comprehensive in my approach as the concept is expansive.
You will read stories about people struggling to align their
lives with their values, as well as those agonizing over writing an equitable will. Interspersed with these more commonly
shared challenges are eclectic tales from the leading edge
about techniques being developed to bequeath tattoos, and

legacy bots that will give us some form of immortality using artificial intelligence.

I foraged for these stories in literary sources and popular media, but I found my real treasure trove of insights in my interviews with dozens of people of all ages. Some of them are living lives that are aligned with their values, and their legacies can be foretold. Others are taking a new life direction or seizing upon unexpected opportunities and can already see the impact they are making. In some cases, the people I interviewed didn't fully grasp the extent of their legacy. They saw themselves as merely doing their best, and recognition was not something they were consciously seeking. In these cases, it was their students, their family members or those they had mentored who testified to their positive and profound influence. In addition, I sought out people who had struggled with the more material aspects of legacy, whether writing their own wills or dealing with the aftermath of someone else's, or being executors of an estate.

My interviews required people to stare unabashedly at their lives. I was asking them to assess whether they had made a difference and to ponder what they would be leaving behind for those they loved—both the good and the bad. Not surprisingly, their responses were often emotionally laden. I was asking them to admit that their lives would end, and to pass judgment on those lives. What had they been putting off for tomorrow—and what if tomorrow never came? Would they regret lives unlived, dreams unfulfilled, amends not made?

I was probing them to think about the responsibilities they might be forced to abandon, including dependent children, parents, siblings or other family members; friends; pets; possessions; business or volunteer commitments. What provisions were they making to fulfill these obligations in their absence? This wasn't idle cocktail party chatter, and sometimes the conversations made people uncomfortable. But people said they had few avenues to speak candidly about their life and their death and, for the most part, they relished the opportunity for these gut-wrenching discussions.

To augment the here and now, I decided to look at the lives of artists—writers, painters and musicians—because they think about history's judgment as part of the creative process. I remembered hearing that Franz Kafka had infamously directed that all his writing be destroyed after his death, and I wondered, with gratitude, why his instructions hadn't been honoured. I had read that the writer and artist Emily Carr had built bonfires to destroy her art and correspondence, and I wanted to know how she had decided what to leave behind. I recalled that the artist Andy Warhol had died unexpectedly in the 1980s after routine surgery, and I was curious whether he'd given any advance thought to the management of his legacy. When I did my homework, I found there were lessons from the legacies of these artists that could apply to us. For additional insight, I talked to professionals who advise people about legacy—lawyers who draw up wills, financial planners who assist with life planning, including legacy gifts, and staff of charities who manage people's donations—and asked them for advice on planning for the inevitable.

The stories recounted in this book were given to me in absolute confidence, and everyone's name has been changed. When you read what these people told me, you'll understand why I've protected their identities. When it came to family secrets, sometimes I was the first person they had told, sometimes the first non-family member. I am very grateful to the interviewees for entrusting me with the intimate details of their lives. Issues of professional confidentiality and personal privacy normally shroud our knowledge of one another's dilemmas around legacy. Thanks to the generosity of my interviewees, we can lift this veil of secrecy. By letting us in on their innermost dilemmas, the contributors are allowing us to gain insights from their struggles and helping us discover solutions to our own problems.

Tears were shed during many interviews for this book, both by the storytellers and the listener. I'm pretty sure you, too, will find their stories moving. When we learn about the pain and joy felt by others, empathy syncs our feelings with theirs. And when their experiences open a vein of connection to our own lives, we also cry for ourselves. Their stories remind us that life is finite and emphasize that what we do with this precious gift matters.

In the next chapters, I explore the many actions we take as we live our lives that will affect our legacy, including embarking on life-affirming initiatives that could have a lasting impact, recording our memoirs, writing our wills, choosing our executors, giving back, passing on our values and sharing our things. Our lives are our legacy, and this book examines all these facets of a multi-sided concept.

But first, let's look at why many of us want to avoid the topic of legacy completely.

Walking with Coffins

We push thoughts of our legacy from our minds because we don't want to face our mortality. There is an evocative Haitian saying that captures our ability to avoid thinking about the grim reaper: "We are all walking with coffins under our arms. Some of us know it and some of us don't." Most of us don't live fully in the moment because we're ignoring that coffin. We've convinced ourselves that we can postpone facing what really matters until some future point in time. If we accepted that our eventual death accompanies our every living moment, we might live with more intensity and give more thought to the kind of imprint we'll be leaving on the earth.

On certain occasions, we're more likely to feel the weight of our coffin. Maybe we have a near-death experience, or someone close to us dies. Sometimes, great art helps us feel the heft of our mortality. During those moments when we accept that our beautiful lives are only on loan, we savour life's sweetness and maybe even squeeze more juice from its fruit. But it's hard to keep that awareness front and centre.

After KS died, I'm certain those of us close to her lived more fully and more consciously—for a while. There were powerful lessons in her death if we chose to learn them. The way she died screamed the alert that it's risky business to postpone living until some future date. She had zero forewarning of her death, so we have to hope that she had already realized her dreams.

And we learned from the way she died that minimizing risk is no safeguard. KS was killed walking her dog on a weekend afternoon on a safe sidewalk in one of the safest neighbourhoods in one of the safest cities in the world. Her stroll and her life ended when a car driven by a drunk driver careened over the curb. And just to belabour the point: this man was already incapacitated by four o'clock in the afternoon when the accident happened—not a normal hour for drunk driving.

When a memorial fund was established in her honour, I wrote our friends to tell them. "I think she would be pleased if I were to pass along as her bequest this parting wish for us all," I wrote. "Don't take it [your life] for granted." Maybe if KS's death caused us to wake up to our own mortality, it wouldn't have been in vain. Maybe this would be some sliver of consolation—a consolation I was longing to find.

We know that some people have a harder time than others thinking about their death. Over half of adult Canadians don't have a will, a statistic that gives us one measure of death avoidance. There are several reasons people don't preplan for their departure that I'll explore later, but some of it is certainly magical thinking: "If I don't think about my death, it won't happen." Or "Writing down my last wishes will trigger my death." People laugh with embarrassment when they confess these thoughts to me. They're afraid of appearing ignorant and superstitious. They needn't worry. When it comes to fear of death, they're in good company.

The award-winning writer Julian Barnes wrote a brilliant book about death called *Nothing to Be Frightened Of*, in which he admits that, contrary to the book's title, he is deathly afraid of death. In his case, the fear is visceral and he describes its manifestations: ". . . from skin-puncturing prod to mind-blanking terror, from the brute alarm bell in the unfamiliar hotel room to klaxons shrieking over the city."[1] Barnes is content with his sense of death and calls it "proportionate." He feels that you cannot begin to understand what life is about unless you are constantly aware of death. "Unless you know and feel that the days of wine and roses are limited, that the wine will madeirize and the roses turn brown in their stinking water before all are thrown out for ever—including the jug—there is no context to such pleasures and interests as come your way on the road to the grave."[2]

While religion and its institutions have always given people opportunities to contemplate death, the secularization of society has left a void. Try discussing mortality at a dinner party and someone is sure to say, "Can't we find a more cheerful topic?" Several ventures have sprung up to fill the gap, including Death Cafés, which offer venues for group-directed chats about death. There is no agenda for these discussions beyond the broad objective "to increase awareness of death with a view to helping people make the most of their (finite) lives." Since 2011, over four thousand Death Cafés have been set up in forty-nine countries across Europe, North America and Australasia. People of all ages attend.[3]

We know from having seen pictures of observances of the Mexican *Día de los Muertos* (Day of the Dead) that cemeteries can be lively places for helping the living cozy up to their mortality and celebrate being alive. The holiday is held during the Feast of All Souls over the first two days of November. Mexicans of all ages dress up as skeletons in fancy dress, festoon graves with flowers and fruits, and feast amidst the tombstones—both to honour their deceased loved ones and to have a great party. Mountain View Cemetery in Vancouver, BC, has launched its own annual All Souls event, complete with candlelit shrines, poetry readings and musical performances. The week-long event is curated by Paula Jardine, the cemetery's artist-in-residence. Cemetery manager Glen Hodges appointed Jardine because he wanted to make the cemetery a place where they did more than just bury the deceased. "This place is about remembering life," he said, "not just about honouring the dead."[4]

Jardine explains why the All Souls event has become a favourite tradition, bringing out crowds. "A lot of young families come here. It's a good way for families to introduce the idea of mortality to children, and a way to remember our ancestors:

our grandparents, our great-grandparents."[5] Activities have included lessons on making sugar skulls, workshops on how to create your own personal shrine, and ceremonial processions led by brass bands.[6]

Some universities are expanding their offerings to include "death classes," courses that explore death from a range of perspectives. The journalist Erika Hayasaki wrote about one of them in her book *The Death Class: A True Story about Life.* The course, Death in Perspective, was taught by Dr. Norma Bowe at Kean University in Union, New Jersey, and had a three-year waiting list. The course included lectures on the biology of dying and field trips to prisons, funeral homes, hospice care centres, mental hospitals and morgues. After watching a dead body being dissected in an autopsy, Bowe often told her students, "It's good to be alive, right? Did you notice how fragile we are? We have no business taking our lives for granted."[7]

One assignment in Bowe's course was for students to focus on their own funeral, including writing their own eulogy, providing detailed instructions to the funeral director regarding disposal of their body, detailing the format of their service and identifying recipients for donations in their memory. Another assignment was to discuss the question "How do the stories of who we are survive our death?" and then write a goodbye letter.

Does all this awareness about death help us focus on our legacy? Dmitri Shostakovich thought so. The composer and pianist suffered from chronic health conditions in his later years, and his final compositions reflect his preoccupation with his own mortality. He concluded that the fear of death is probably the deepest feeling we have and that it galvanizes us to perform with an eye to our posterity. "The irony lies in the fact that under the influence of that fear [of death] people create poetry, prose and music; that is, they try to strengthen their ties with the living and increase their influence on them," he wrote.[8]

We are surrounded by examples of the extraordinary things people achieve when they know their lives will be fore-shortened. By the time brain cancer cut short Gord Downie's life in 2017 when he was fifty-three, he had left a remarkable legacy. The composer and lead singer for the Canadian rock band The Tragically Hip devoted the last years of his life to telling the story of Chanie Wenjack, a twelve-year-old Ojibwe boy who, in 1966, ran away from a residential school in northern Ontario and died of exposure while trying to walk six hundred kilometres home to his family. Downie created the multimedia project *Secret Path* for people to learn about Wenjack's heart-rending fate and to help them understand the terrible legacy of the residential school system. The project included an album, which Downie and his band per-formed in sell-out concerts across Canada, a graphic novel, and an animated film broadcast on TV and shared in community screenings across the country.

Downie knew his death was imminent and this mission galvanized him. As his brother Mike Downie said, "It's fill-ing him up. He's not looking back. He's looking forward and he's busy living right now."[9] The Gord Downie & Chanie

Wenjack Fund has been established to remember Wenjack and continue Downie's commitment to improving the lives of indigenous people.[10]

Our lives are our legacies, and we will be remembered for the way we lived. Catastrophic illness or injury, as in the case of Gord Downie, can propel people to accomplish their goals in a foreshortened time frame. But what about the rest of us—we who also will die but have not been given the end date? The next chapter tells the stories of people who were going about their daily business when something pushed them in a new direction. Their stories are a reminder that while we are breathing, we are shaping our legacy, and it is wise to keep taking our own measure to ensure we are who we want to be.

Changing Our Lives

The Greek philosopher Socrates argued that the unexamined life is not worth living. But it's what comes after the examination that really matters. The Death in Perspective course assignment to write our own eulogies is an effective technique for reminding us that our lives are our legacies, and that both our lives and our legacies are in perpetual development. The exercise of eulogy writing allows us to present our case and tell our story in a way that will make us proud of the life we have lived to date, or at least make our decisions understandable and our choices comprehensible. But in trying to mount our defence, we might find our legacy wanting. We might be compelled to forge the material for a new eulogy. We might decide to change our lives. This chapter looks at the examples of one fictional character and four real people who were driven to undertake personal transformations, each propelled by very different motivations. In every case, the result was a more impactful legacy.

The Conversion of Ebenezer Scrooge

When we think about transformations, it's hard to beat the electrifying conversion of Ebenezer Scrooge, the monumental character created by Charles Dickens in *A Christmas Carol*. Scrooge begins the tale as an "odious, stingy, hard, unfeeling man."[1] By the time the story wraps up, he is "as good a friend, as good a master, and as good a man, as the good old city knew, or any other good old city, town or borough, in the good old world."[2] One reason Scrooge becomes a reformed man is that the Ghost of Christmas Yet to Come allows him to preview his death—and in his case, there was no eulogy. Scrooge views his corpse on his deathbed "plundered and bereft, unwatched, unwept, uncared for."[3] He mourns his own fate, and he also recognizes his role in the death foretold of dear Tiny Tim, the crippled son of his badly treated employee. When Scrooge is given the chance to change his legacy, he seizes it.

The story *A Christmas Carol* is well known, and when I ask friends and family to recount the tale, they focus on Scrooge's late-in-life rehabilitation. What they are less likely to remember is that this was actually Scrooge's second major life transformation. His first was changing from a young man with fine ambitions who had earned the hand of a loving young woman, to the covetous, hard-hearted Scrooge. When the Ghost of Christmas Past takes Scrooge back in time to see himself as a young man in his prime, his face has "begun to wear the signs of care and avarice" and in his eye, there is "an eager, greedy, restless motion."[4]

Scrooge is forced to revisit the moment when his fair young fiancée calls off their engagement. She tells Scrooge that she has watched the idol of greed displace her in his heart. She says she is freeing Scrooge from his commitment to her because she foresees a time when he will regret having married her because she does not have a dowry. "I have seen your nobler aspirations fall off one by one, until the master-passion, Gain, engrosses you . . . You *are* changed. When it [our contract] was made, you were another man."[5] She leaves Scrooge with the parting wish that he be happy in the life he has chosen. The ghost then makes Scrooge witness the happy life his ex-fiancée subsequently made for herself—a life filled with love and laughter, boisterous children and an adoring husband—a vision that overwhelms Scrooge with regret for what might have been.

A Christmas Carol was first published in 1843, but its theme is completely contemporary. Recently, a young woman we'll call Sarah, who could be a stand-in for Scrooge's fair young fiancée, played out an eerily similar scenario with her boyfriend of several years. They were living together and everyone assumed they would marry. But Sarah found that her boyfriend was spending more and more time on his business ventures and less and less time with her. "Whenever one of his commercial projects wrapped up," Sarah says, "I hoped our life would rebalance. But then another corporate priority would reclaim first place in his life." Sarah loved her boyfriend but wanted something more, for both of them. Finally, she worked up the courage to face the problem. When she confronted her

Scrooge, he, like his fictional counterpart, did not disagree with her assessment. He claimed that his priority, for now, had to be his career. He walked away from the relationship and gave Sarah up. With this decision, they are both writing their legacies on different trajectories.

Bridging the Chasm

In her book *The Call of Character: Living a Life Worth Living*, Mari Ruti, professor of critical thinking, sees our character, our personal truth, as always in the making. She says that finding our authentic self is a question "of bridging the chasm between our current reality and what we have the potential to become."[6] Haida artist Bill Reid is an eloquent example of someone who was able to bridge the chasm. When Reid died in 1998 at the age of seventy-eight, he left behind a profoundly influential legacy as a renowned artist and activist whose work as a goldsmith, sculptor, carver, painter, writer and an advocate garnered international recognition. After beginning his career as a broadcaster and part-time jeweller, Reid gradually forged his professional path through an accumulation of decisions made over decades. His inner transformation over this period was even more profound: Reid became Haida.

This inner transformation is what extended Reid's legacy beyond his own unforgettable artwork, although that would have been impact enough. The anthropologist George MacDonald posits that Reid's yellow cedar carving *The Raven and the First*

Men, housed in the heart of the Museum of Anthropology at UBC, is one of the holiest of holy places in Canada.[7] This powerful work depicts a massive raven atop a clamshell from which small humans are struggling to emerge. The image is unforgettable and its impact is enhanced by its placement atop an old gun turret left over from World War II. As the architect of the museum, Arthur Erickson, wrote, "The gun turret, the symbol of war, base for destruction, was to be vanquished by his [Reid's] haunting portrayal of Creation."[8] The Canadian government has acknowledged the significance of this sculpture by reproducing its image on a twenty-dollar banknote.

While Reid was perfecting his own brilliant artwork, he became a celebrant of Haida creative expression and actively worked to promote Haida culture and protect Haida land. In the process, he came to realize that this was *his* culture and *his* land. But that process was gradual. "I was actually in my early teens before I even became conscious of the fact that I was anything other than an average Caucasian North American," Reid wrote.[9] He had been raised in largely white communities and his father was an American of German and Scottish descent. But both his mother and grandmother were Haida, and in that culture, this matrilineal lineage made him Haida too.

Reid's biographer Doris Shadbolt wrote that Reid's central driving passion was to be Haida in more than blood. He wanted to be "an aware and conscious Haida with the inner assurance of identity and knowledge and the sense of community that that meant."[10] Over the years, his engagement with

Haida culture encompassed many spheres as he fought for recognition of the universal value of Haida art and the need to
protect the Haida culture, including supporting anti-logging
campaigns on Haida Gwaii, part of the Haida traditional territory. Miles Richardson, a citizen of the Haida Nation who has
played key government roles in treaty and land issues in BC,
sums up Reid's legacy: "We, the Haida Nation—and, I believe,
humankind—are better off because he did accept that part of
himself, that important identity that he was an heir to. He put
the best he had into living it and bringing it forward."[11]

Destiny Descends like a Force of Nature

Whereas Reid came to his legacy as a gradual process, other people have their destiny descend upon them like a force of nature.
The Persian poet Rumi was thirty-seven years old when the
sixty-year-old wandering dervish Shams of Tabriz derailed his
life and forged his future. Rumi owes his universal stature to his
life-altering collision with Shams. Here's how Rumi described
Shams's impact: "When your love enflamed my heart all I had
was burned to ashes, except your love. I put logic and learning
and books on the shelf."[12] Rumi's love for Shams was to find
expression in a breathtaking outpouring of lyrical verse that has
been translated into many languages, immortalizing Rumi as
one of the world's most-read poets, and one of its most admired.

The year of their meeting was 1244 and the place was Konya,
in present-day Turkey. At his relatively young age, Rumi was
already a leader in his community, a powerful and popular preacher,

and a respected religious scholar with academic appointments. As the story goes, Rumi was going about his business, astride a mule, surrounded by a retinue of followers forming a reverential procession. Shams, a stranger, recently arrived and dressed in an unprepossessing coarse black felt cloak, grabbed the reins of Rumi's mule and engaged him in a short, almost blasphemous, theological exchange. From this first meeting, their lives became briefly but intensely interwoven. Rumi's biographer Brad Gooch calculated that their relationship covered a period of only about two and a half years, and Shams disappeared for a year of that time. But they spent nine months "in near seclusion night and day as they communed, talked, and shared secrets."[13]

Shams's mission was to illuminate Rumi's heart. As Rumi set aside logic and learning and books, Shams replaced them with music, sung poetry and dancing—most famously, the spinning of the whirling dervishes. Gooch explains that when Shams was instructing Rumi in whirling, he was teaching him "to literally spin loose of language and logic, while opening and warming his heart."[14] The story ends tragically with Shams's disappearance. He left without saying goodbye, and he and Rumi never saw one another again. Rumi spent years searching for Shams but found no trace. There is suspicion that Shams was murdered by people jealous of his influence over Rumi. The separation nearly drove Rumi mad, but he turned his grief into a creative outpouring of odes and quatrains titled *The Works of Shams of Tabriz*.

Thanks to Shams's transformative influence, Rumi found his voice and became the groundbreaking poet whose work still speaks to us hundreds of years after his death. According to Gooch, the poems Rumi wrote "moved beyond anything dared so far in either Persian lyric poetry or Muslim devotional poetry."[15] Rumi's highly respected translator Coleman Barks described his first encounter with the poems as being similar to the love-at-first-sight of Rumi and Shams: "I felt such an opening of my heart, a sense of reckless longing, an expansion of my sense of what's possible in a poem, and in a life."[16]

Change as a Wake-Up Call

Most people don't cross paths with a Shams of Tabriz who rocks their world. More likely, they'll wake up one day and decide to change their own life—or at least it feels that way. The decision is more likely the culmination of a complicated and gradual thought process. But there is often a trigger that pushes them over the edge. In Meredith's case, it was leaving her twenties. "Four years ago, when I turned thirty," Meredith recalls, "I decided it was time for a radical redirection." She was working in a fast-paced Asian city in a well-paid, high-powered job, and living with her talented, athletic husband. You can imagine her as a model for one of those airline ads, the beautiful young executive on the move, with the world as her oyster. "I liked my life," she says. "My job came with a very nice paycheque, and I could even argue I was doing something socially useful by helping governments raise money for worthwhile public projects. We did exciting things and we were having a lot of fun."

But a number of things began to nag at her. "I was starting to become irritated by the superficial focus on material things that surrounded me. Even our biking group turned what should have been a fitness exercise into a competition for the latest gear. I had always thought I didn't care about money, but I worried I was changing. I knew deep down I needed to keep searching for what was right for me. I kept thinking I'd make a change in another year—but then another year would come and go."

"That thirtieth birthday was the turning point," she says. "I felt I couldn't let another year go by. It wasn't any one thing that pushed me to action, it was more an accumulation of factors. Both my husband and I were working way too hard. We didn't have enough time to spend together, and this was starting to affect our relationship. We had always talked about having children and we couldn't make that work with the lives we had." So, Meredith decided to veer off in a new direction, and she ended up returning to her roots. "My husband and I moved back to the sleepy small city where I'd grown up," she says, "and I completely turned my life around." Four years later, Meredith has two little children, works reasonable hours in a small company and lives near her parents, her sister and her sister's family. "Even my brother recently moved back from overseas," she says. "We all separated after high school and are now gathering back here again." As a completely unexpected bonus, Meredith has just received an award for her contributions to her professional community.

Looking back, Meredith feels that her decision to return to basics was about building a legacy for her unborn children. "I wanted my children to grow up in this place," she says, "and I wanted them to have these kinds of values. I wanted them to know their family and experience the outdoors. My husband is seven years older than me, and his father died when he was three years old, so I was thinking about that. Now, if I were to die, my family has a home here—somewhere for them to be grounded. It would not have been like that in Asia, where they wouldn't have had a support group or any history connecting them to the culture."

Meredith confesses there's something else that has made her more conscious of life's fragility. Before leaving Asia, she was a witness to a bar brawl that ended with a man being brutally murdered. "We were at a resort when some local men randomly targeted a vacationer," she recalls. "He fell to the floor and they smashed chairs on him and slit his throat with a broken bottle. I think anyone who experiences a horror like this must be changed in some way. Now I have a will. I have life insurance. I know this isn't common for someone my age. But when this poor man walked into that bar, he never knew he wouldn't come out alive."

Change Forced upon Us

A few years before the death of my dear friend KS, illness forced a life change upon her. She turned the ordeal into an opportunity to expand, deepen and strengthen her bonds with her family, her friends and her community. Before her illness, she had been living the life of the classic overstretched divorced mom with primary responsibility for her two young sons and a career with demands that never let up. She was one of the few senior women in her office in an era before programs like flex hours to accommodate child care, and she had no support structure at home. Her children were entering the teen years and needed her. Add to this her drive for perfection and her obsession with giving one hundred percent to every task, and you knew something had to give.

I was increasingly distressed at the visible toll these demands were taking on KS, and I became a relentless nag about the need to put herself first. I found a letter she'd written to me about seven years before her death, apparently after one of my pep talks. She thanked me for my good advice and vowed to post an "advice list" to herself on the fridge. Her list included the following: "Ask for (demand from kids) help; schedule breaks, withdraw; exercise; sleep." This was too little, too late. Her headaches became debilitating migraines, the kind where you spend hours throwing up or lying in a darkened room praying for release. The doctor gave her this layman's explanation of her illness: "You've had your accelerator pressed to the floor for so long, your body has forgotten how to release it. You're always in overdrive and can't gear down." A plethora of treatments and strategies were prescribed, but they offered little relief. KS became so unwell that her doctor insisted she take medical leave from work.

Her transition from accomplished career woman to person on sick leave was not easy. She felt like a failure and worried she was letting her colleagues down. I kept reminding her that she had already overpaid her dues to the work world. I argued that her accomplishments were legendary, and she could afford to rest on her laurels and concentrate on more pressing priorities. Plus, she had no choice. She had to follow her doctor's orders.

This forced withdrawal from her demanding profession proved to be a godsend. KS took her boundless energy and brilliant mind and redirected them to immediate needs—her own health and well-being, and that of her family and her community. During this period, I recall her being worried about her teenage son's state of mind. She began taking naps so she would be able to stay up and talk to him after he rolled home in the wee hours of the morning. During those late-night gabfests, she said, they talked about everything under the sun. She was certain those conversations were what saw him through a rough patch. At least they kept her from going insane with worry. If she hadn't been on sick leave, she couldn't have maintained this punishing schedule.

This gift of a new dawn was made more precious by the fact that, unbeknownst to KS, only a few years remained of her treasured life. The biggest impact of her life change was that she began very deliberately and consciously to stop and smell the roses. She wrote to me about this process and wanted me to know that she had "stopped taking our friendship for granted." The delightful result was that she pushed me to find more time to spend with her. We shared a hiking adventure to the mountains, cross-country ski outings, road trips and general good times. And I was just one of the many friends with whom she shared her new-found philosophy. Most significantly, she had the time to pour love and caring and wisdom into her teenage sons. They were so satiated by her devotion that when she died, although they deeply mourned her loss, they were able to say that she had given them everything they could possibly need. As well, her freshly minted celebration of life opened her to the possibility of a new intimate relationship, and she fell in love and got engaged. At the funeral, her younger son said that one of the things that gave him comfort was that his mother died "ridiculously happy" due to her pending marriage to the love of her life.

Before her life change, KS's impressive professional legacy was carved in stone. After redirecting her life, KS expanded and deepened this legacy: by preparing her boys for a motherless future, by strengthening the impact she was having in her community, and by leaving an indelible mark on her friends and family. As you'll read later, these investments of time and energy have lived on.

The stories of Ebenezer Scrooge, Bill Reid, Rumi, Meredith and KS are powerful arguments to live consciously and find a pathway to our unique contribution—before our life runs out. As Rumi says, "Don't be satisfied with stories, how things have gone with others. Unfold your own myth."[17]

The people whose stories you just read veered dramatically from their life course. But there are other ways to unfold our own myth that may not require such abrupt departures from the path we are on. Impactful legacies can be created by the accumulation of daily purposeful actions. As you'll read in the next chapter, sometimes people stay their course and just dig deeper. Sometimes they open themselves to opportunities they can incorporate into their current trajectory. Sometimes they align with others to amplify the impact.

Living Our Legacies

The stories in this chapter are about people who are forging their legacy day by day by aligning their values with their daily lives. Some have linked their day jobs with their goal of giving back, others are making a difference in their spare time. Some began fulfilling their life purpose as employees and have carried on as volunteers. Their examples remind us that sometimes you don't need to change your life to find your legacy; you just need to pay attention.

Improving Your Own Backyard

Blair has followed the principle of improving his own backyard his entire life, beginning as a junior forest warden in his preteens and continuing to pursue forestry as a career and a passion. "I was building a legacy without really knowing it," he says. "I didn't have a long-range plan. It was more inspirational." Right after Blair graduated from university, he was looking for work and landed what he saw as "an unbelievable opportunity." A new job in forest recreation opened up with the government to establish a system of recreation sites and trails across the province. Blair's job was to get the program up and running, and now, decades later, he estimates there are 3,500 recreation reserves. He can see the results of his work every time he runs across happy hikers or enthusiastic camping families.

At age fifty-eight, Blair retired from his forestry career but simply switched to the volunteer side of the same commitment. "We moved to a new community where I found that volunteerism was thriving. I got introduced to the local residents' association and it's been the focus of my life for the past fifteen years. Our first project was removing invasive species from the last remaining green space in our area. By the time the space was designated as a park, volunteers had spent 4,500 hours in the invasive species removal project. It took us five years to get the park designation and we had to participate in public meetings to stop a condo development."

His next project, which focused on restoring another park, earned Blair and his group of volunteers an environmental award. "My official title is volunteer project steward," says Blair. The award acknowledged Blair's leadership as "inspirational" and lauded the group for tipping the balance of the ecological health of the area while, at the same time, having a great deal of fun.

Blair has recently been diagnosed with Parkinson's and he has informed his team of his illness. "Our estimation is that we have another five years to complete the project, so we have a target," he says. "My job is to set the parameters for the work.

If something happens to me, others might take on my role, but it also might become more of a shared responsibility."

When I ask Blair how his team has responded to his illness, he chokes up. "The group is quietly supportive of me," he says. "I notice they now carry the heavy loads. I don't find otherwise that things are very different. There is more awareness of the need for the team to expand its numbers and become more inclusive of new members, and I see this as part of my legacy. We are one of the biggest volunteer groups in the area and we should be able to continue to grow. Stewardship of a natural area is a perfect place to leave your legacy. You can see the results."

Surf Sisters

When Shelley Renard moved to Tofino, BC, in 1977, she became one of the first women to surf the huge, ice-cold rollers of the Pacific Northwest. Soon, other surfing women joined her and they began to set records. They also put the remote town of two thousand residents on the map for surfers worldwide, especially the surfing sorority. By doing what they love, they are leaving a legacy of female empowerment, athletic achievement and environmental stewardship.

Renard learned to surf at age twenty-three and broke into the tight men's club by showing she could hold her own. Four decades later, what was once a pretty solitary female activity in Tofino is now a surfing sisterhood of many dedicated women and girls. One of the leading lights is Catherine Bruhwiler,

Canada's first professional female surfer, who has won the women's Canadian national surfing champion title many times and competes with Team Canada in international events. The younger generation of athletes is represented by Mathea Olin, a fifteen-year-old Olympic hopeful.[1] Josie Osborne, mayor of Tofino, describes her town as having a "surfer girl culture" and notes that one surfing competition saw a three-to-one ratio of girls to boys in the under-sixteen and under-twelve divisions. She says one reason the girls in town have a "can-do" attitude is the "many positive role models—lots of people like Catherine Bruhwiler."[2]

To further encourage women and girls to discover the sport, Tofino boasts a surfing school called Surf Sister, where the instructors are all female. The school, now the biggest all-female-instructor surf school in the world, was founded in 1999 with the vision "to encourage more women to try surfing and to have them feel less intimidated and feel included out in the water."[3] In 2009, Surf Sister spearheaded Queen of the Peak, an all-women surf competition. More than one hundred women and children have competed for cash and prizes in the three-day competition, which provides free child care. The 2017 winners included participants from California and Florida/Hawaii, as well as Tofino.[4]

About fifteen years ago, Sam Goski took a course at Surf Sister. Today, she owns Gyro Beach Board Shop and Yew Tree Yoga in Victoria, BC, separate businesses operating from the same building as a testament to the overlapping nature of the practices. Sam and her team provide lessons in stand-up paddle boarding and instruction in yoga, and Sam has her own physio-therapist practice. Today, we're familiar with this concept of integrating yoga and paddleboards, but a decade and a half ago, this wasn't such an obvious fit, and Sam got her bolt of insight from Surf Sister. She vividly remembers the day when these two concepts married themselves in her mind. "It was a spec-tacularly beautiful spring day and we students were sitting on the beach with our surfing instructor," Sam recalls. "I had been given the day lesson as a gift, so I'd taken time away from my physio practice to make my way to Tofino, and I didn't know what to expect. That first moment on the beach was in many ways the most memorable of the course for me. I was taken aback at the beautiful posture of our instructor as she sat in a cross-legged pose on the beach. I was a physiotherapist and, despite being so body conscious, I couldn't replicate her easy alignment. I thought, 'She must have a serious yoga practice.' Watching the way this fine athlete moved her body planted some seeds that left a big legacy."

Returning to our female surfing pioneer, Shelley Renard, we find her, four decades later, in a day job at a preschool, where she continues her passion, teaching. From April to June, Renard organizes surf lessons for the kindergarten class. The children are taught about riptides and currents and learn to overcome any fear of the water. They also learn the signif-icance of being good stewards of nature and the importance of keeping the ocean clean. Renard describes these classes as "getting out there and utilizing our resources," referring to the ocean.[5] Renard's commitment will bring along the next generation, and the passion of the surf sisters will keep making waves.

Game Changer

Sometimes your legacy creeps up on you. You pursue a passion and while doing something you love, you end up changing people's lives. This happened to Santiago when he decided to follow his girlfriend to her job in Africa. For the previous two years, they had often been apart, working in their countries of origin, but had managed to keep their relationship alive despite the challenges. Now they were determined to live together in a new country, but to do this, Santiago needed an entry visa. Good fortune arrived in the form of a non-profit organization that recruited Santiago as a volunteer. He was twenty-nine years old when he arrived in Africa. When he departed nearly three years later, his significant contribution was acknowledged with a trophy in his honour.

Santiago's day job was working as a volunteer with several non-profit organizations as a construction and maintenance manager. But his dream was to use his spare time to learn to play rugby. He had never played the game before but hoped that his passion for sports would open the door. He was both surprised and disappointed to find that, despite being surrounded by rugby-playing countries, this one had no tradition of the game. But the first week after he arrived, he saw a poster recruiting people for a rugby team and he added his name and phone number to the list.

The beginnings of what was to become both a national rugby team and a countrywide commitment to the sport consisted of the dozen people who responded to the poster. The man who circulated the poster was a seasoned rugby player—and the only one who knew anything about the game. The novices held their first three rugby practices on a tennis court, concentrating on running and passing drills with no tackling. Then they expanded to twenty people and graduated to an indoor basketball court. Santiago describes the uphill battle: "I learned about how to play my position from the drills and watching videos, and after about three months, we had our first game. It was the first time I grabbed the ball in an official play and learned what it was like to be tackled. We lost that first game but we got an idea of how to play rugby."

The team was determined to improve. They practised three times per week, travelled outside the country for games and continued playing tournaments through the off-season. They graduated to practising on a school sports field. A rival national team from a neighbouring country admired their spunk, offered them training courses and gave them manuals to teach them the fundamentals. Rugby is a tough game, especially if your opponents are bigger, tougher and more experienced, and Santiago's team got a lot of injuries. Santiago himself suffered a broken hand and a split forehead.

"We didn't win a single game in the first season," he says, "but we kept getting better and better, and the country was becoming more passionate about the sport." Their initial team was joined by a university team, and then a team formed by the police, until there were four tournament teams with about forty people playing. This critical mass led to the establishment of an official national rugby team with sponsorships from local companies that paid for essentials like uniforms.

Five years have passed since Santiago signed his name to that recruitment poster, and the countrywide adoption of the game of rugby is remarkable in its scope. The national men's league has been joined by a national women's league, and both girls and boys have an under-eighteen tournament and an under-twelve tournament. There are over one hundred schools with rugby as an official sport, offering both skills training and the league games. As for the national team, they've been required by the international rugby league to jump up to the next division because they're severely trouncing the lower-ranking opponents. Before Santiago left the country, the national league dedicated three trophies to the original founders. The cup in Santiago's name is awarded every year to the team that comes in second in the tournament.

Santiago can see the impact of the sport's contribution. "Right from the beginning, the players became very dedicated," he says. "They got into the routine of exercise and getting in shape. To play well, you need to be sober and have good nutrition and drink a lot of water. Excelling at this sport can give people different options in life. Maybe they can get a scholar-ship, or other educational opportunities will open up. And then there's the pride people have in the players and in their own capacity. It has been amazing to watch rugby become so much more than just a game." Santiago has continued to support the team at a distance by managing their social media, and his goal is to return someday to help develop a marketing and fundraising strategy. "Rugby is making a big contribution right now, but the potential is unlimited," he says. His commitment to learning a new sport sparked an entire country's passion, and he leaves a legacy of community engagement and athletic excellence.

Science Educator and Environmental Steward

Bob retired nine years ago at age fifty-five from his job as a high school science teacher. He had taught for thirty-one years and had been in the same high school for thirty of those years. "This was the right time for me to retire," Bob says. "I was able to pass the torch. One of my former students replaced me as the chemistry teacher." He says that watching life come full circle has been one of the really satisfying things about his career. "Students I taught in my first years of teaching became teachers themselves and are now returning to the school. I know of four former students who have become chemistry teachers. One dad says I inspired his daughter to become a doctor. He says she was a social science person until she took biology from me."

Since his retirement, Bob has spent countless hours volun-teering on environmental projects, some of which he started with his students when he was still teaching, including an environment leadership program, a fish hatchery and a watershed monitoring program. Other projects focus on restoring the native forest in the region by cultivating trees that are hardy to diseases that threaten their species. He has worked with a variety of organizations at all levels—from chairing the board and fundraising, to day-to-day cleanup.

"One of my projects is with a nearby three-hundred-acre wildlife management area," Bob says. "I'm one of only two full-time volunteers, and the other man is eighty-seven years old and can't physically help me. I meet with the public, but I also do the lawn-cutting, fix the drains, clean the washrooms, remove the garbage and empty the donation boxes. Every year, I organize a team of volunteers to teach the public about a bird migration that lasts about a month."

Bob has big plans for the future, including expanding the trail program and improving the signage, developing a program for co-op students, and partnering with other organizations. "On spaceship earth, there are no passengers; only crew," he says. "You'll never live long enough to see the results of what you're working on, so you're doing it for your children and your grandchildren. It's better to light the candle than curse in the dark. Act locally. Improve your own backyard." Bob's lifelong commitment to his own backyard has inspired others to follow in his footsteps, and his legacy is paying daily dividends to his fellow citizens and to Mother Nature.

Designing a Business to Give Back

Two years ago, a friend of Kate's made her a job offer that was the perfect fit—it would combine her skills and her interests with her passion for giving back. Kate was thirty-three years old and working as a full-time illustrator with an educational publisher. She had no desire to leave her day job but she wanted more. Kate's friend had a philanthropic business idea and wanted Kate to come aboard as a creative partner. And she could do the job "in her spare time." The concept was to create a sports clothing company that would encourage people to engage in athletic activities and, at the same time, would provide financial assistance to sports programs for children. The clothing would be Canadian-designed and Canadian-made and, for every garment sold, the company would donate a percentage to initiatives that created opportunities for more Canadian children to play sports.

"It all started with the idea that physical activity is integral to human health and wellness," Kate says, "while recognizing that many Canadian families face financial barriers that make it more difficult for kids to play organized sports. Being involved in youth athletics lays a strong foundation for an active lifetime, with far-reaching benefits for our bodies and minds, as well as our social and personal development."

Kate remembers what drew her to the opportunity. "I always feel happiest and most at harmony with the world when I am helping make other people happy or improving their quality of life," she says. "In my day job, I'm removed from seeing how my work positively impacts the world. I don't get to see students experiencing that 'ah-ha' moment when the illustration I created helps them understand a difficult concept. I know that happens, but I don't get to see it first-hand. Both my business partner and I have personally benefited from our experiences with sports, and we want to use our athletic clothing company to harness this power to give back."

Kate's job with the company is creating the clothing designs and developing content for social media and marketing. "Building this company has been a wonderful opportunity to use my illustration and design skills to do some good in the world," she says. "I am also learning so much about running a socially conscious business, not only in terms of our efforts to give back, but also ethically sourcing our manufacturing partners in Canada, and partnering with other businesses whose philosophies and actions align with our own."

Kate's motivation to make athletic activities more inclusive is fuelled by her childhood experiences. "I was able to participate in various school sports as a kid," she says, "which helped me become a little less shy. Then, as a teen, I discovered horseback riding. Although it wasn't always easy financially, with the help of my very resourceful parents, I was able to live out this passion, which has brought more joy to my life than I could have imagined. As an adult, I have rediscovered a love for running, particularly on beautiful nature trails, and am currently enjoying training for my fourth marathon." Kate feels that all of these athletic experiences have shaped her into the person she is today and have connected her with great people. "Living an active lifestyle continues to support my physical and mental health," she says. "My hopes are that through our company, we can help open similar doors for children in our communities."

The two partners have since gained a third and are working as a team to build their dream of a Canadian athletic clothing company that gives back. "It has been a big challenge to balance my full-time illustration job with starting a business," Kate admits. "But knowing that we are making a positive impact in the lives of many children keeps me engaged in the work. Running also helps keep me balanced by releasing stress in a positive way and clears my mind for more creative ideas to come alive. Sometimes I'm overwhelmed thinking about all of the good that the world still needs. But I'm comforted by a quote from the musician Jana Stanfield: 'I cannot do all the good that the world needs. But the world needs all the good that I can do.'"

In this chapter, we've looked at people who are leaving a significant legacy by participating in community or countrywide change. Thanks to them, environments are being improved, sport cultures are being transformed, and barriers to athletic participation are being lowered. Their contributions will continue to resonate long after they've gone.

In the next chapter, we get down close and look at the ways we make change person by person and live on in the people whose lives we've touched.

Leaving Ourselves in Others

We leave our legacy by giving of ourselves in our relationships, and we achieve immortality in the memories of those we've influenced and through their ongoing actions. We are standing on the shoulders of those who have gone before us, and we hope to provide that foundation to the generations that follow. This chapter looks at people who have had a profound impact on others and explores how they too were influenced. There's a high school teacher who opened the minds of his students, a grandmother who inspires her grandchildren, a mentor and a young man who engage in mutual give and take, and a homeless philosopher who forged deep bonds with his community. Their stories remind us that we are surrounded by opportunities to leave ourselves in others, and encourage us to leave our legacy through this gift of connection.

Teacher

When teachers transmit information, skills, attitudes, values and the sheer love of learning, they leave their imprint on their students. They are in a key position to have an immediate influence on their students' lives and can leave legacies that reverberate from generation to generation. This has been the case with a high school teacher we'll call Steve. Here, four of Steve's former students who were in his classroom half a century ago look back on his impact. Their stories illustrate the power of an exemplary teacher to leave an indelible mark on other human beings.

Steve began crafting his legacy at age twenty-two. That's when he entered classroom 9B and introduced himself to a couple of dozen teenagers as their English teacher. Four former students, now in their late sixties, can describe with remarkable clarity the impact this young man had on them. All of them have incorporated the arts into their lives in major ways, and three are published authors. All four say they learned from Steve lifelong lessons about questioning conventional thinking. The two women have had careers that defied the gender expectations of a small-town mentality. And the two men are living openly gay lives, and have done so for decades, after coming out in an era that was less accepting than today's.

Steve was a gifted teacher and his passion for his subject was contagious. "In Steve's class, literature was presented with reverence and delight," Alison remembers, "rather than as something to study so we could pass an exam. His background in theatre showed in his engaging teaching style, and I absorbed every word he said. He ignited my lifelong love of books and reading." Steve's influence would prove to be life-changing for Alison. She remembers the exact moment when he set in motion her literary career. "One day, he asked the class if anyone wanted to be a writer," she remembers. "I was too timid to announce that yes, I did. But he pointed to me and said, 'You could be a writer.' I was thrilled he thought so. But then he added, 'You could succeed because you have discipline, and that's the most important thing.' At the time, this puzzled me. But much later, I realized he was right—talent and creativity will only get you so far. If you don't have discipline, you won't ever finish a book. Over the years, as I struggled with not getting published and almost giving up, I remembered his words and kept going. The fact that he had seen a possibility in me made all the difference." Alison is now an award-winning writer. Her books have been published in several languages and her stories have appeared in anthologies, newspapers and magazines.

Richard is another of Steve's students who has made an outstanding contribution to the arts. "I dreamed of being an actor and playwright from age five," he says. "Steve is one of the key people who gave me the confidence to make my dream a reality. My reminiscences from high school are full of examples of Steve's life lessons—like the way his grit kept us all together when the opening night of our musical had to be cancelled and rescheduled because of the leading lady's stage fright." Richard is an award-winning and internationally acclaimed playwright and novelist, and his friendship with Steve continues to this day. "Steve's enthusiasm and ever-eager optimism continue to brighten my life," Richard says.

Beyond transmitting a deep love of his subject, Steve excelled at pushing young people to expand their horizons. "I will always be grateful," Alison says, "at a time when conformity was expected, especially for girls, that he encouraged us to question conventional thinking and to explore the world beyond our sleepy, conservative city." Joan says this was Steve's biggest impact on her. "From an early age, I was determined to find some new territory that was off our tiny map of possible girl futures," she says. "I remember vividly a dramatic exchange with Steve that crystallized my commitment. One day, when high school and our time with Steve was drawing to a close, he decided to really push us. It was like a final life exam. One by one, he told each of us what our future would look like if we didn't apply ourselves. When he introduced the exercise, I thought it was pretty risky because it was so personal. But he'd been our teacher all these years, and I felt he'd earned the right to give us his opinion. Plus, I was very curious to hear what he had to say. His comments about every one of us were very insightful and I remember a lot of laughter. When it came to me, he said that if I didn't apply myself, I'd 'marry well' and spend my days chairing volunteer committees. I remember my response was vehement. 'I'll prove you wrong.' It was all very theatrical and I don't believe there was ever a real danger of me not pursuing a career. But I never forgot our exchange. I loved proving him wrong—and I like to think it pleased him too."

Joan remembers Steve's disruptive techniques as a feature of his effective teaching style. "He encouraged us to throw our preconceptions out the window," she says. "He would lean against the grey window ledge and ask questions such as 'Why are you certain the sun will rise tomorrow?' One day, we showed up to class and our chairs were in a circle. This technique may be commonplace now, but it was heresy in the days of regimented desk rows. We were shocked and delighted."

Gregory also remembers these techniques as an integral part of Steve's teaching strategy. "Discourse and debate were profoundly encouraged by Steve," he says. "He gave me room to explore their power and he nurtured my love of language and made it flourish. He was singularly responsible for my love of theatre. My involvement with the world of theatre began with him and continues to this day." Gregory feels the greatest impact Steve had on his life was as a male role model. "Back in high school, I didn't realize I was gay, but I was profoundly influenced by Steve as a representative of the adult world who played the world differently," he says. "He showed me an adult male role very different from other male figures in my life, whether in the school world or the public world. He both conveyed and allowed a sensitivity, a femininity that was way off the norm in our conservative town."

Steve's legacy is huge, particularly when you consider that these are the views of a handful of his students and he had a thirty-three-year teaching career. In addition, he was able to continue his influence after he retired, spending a couple of decades running theatre productions with young people. So, to say that I saw the tip of his legacy iceberg is a major understatement. Why was he able to have such an impact? He was clearly a skilled and committed teacher, but there seem to be other factors that supported his character moulding. First, he had a receptive audience in class 9B. This "Special English" class gathered together students with the inclination and aptitude to really dig into his topics. And during their high school careers, they had a surprising amount of exposure to Steve and his world view. "I spent a lot of hours with this class," he recalls. "Over a four-year period, I taught them literature and composition. So that meant they had eight English classes every week with me, plus two exams. I was also their homeroom teacher." And some of them participated in his theatrical productions. Steve remembers the class of 9B fondly. "They were my very first teaching class," he says, "and I can even tell you where individual students sat in the classroom."

Steve had a mission. "I felt the parents had carved a moat around their children to protect them," he says. "I wanted them to go out and believe in themselves. They were like a bottle of Coke. After you shake the bottle, it still looks the same. But then you lift the top off and away it goes."

When I remind Steve what his students have accomplished and how they feel about his contribution, he is quick to minimize his role. "I've always been serious about not taking credit for the achievement of kids I've taught," he says. "If they give you credit that's one thing, but to grab it is wrong. I think a lot of people want to take credit for those who achieve highly. If I've been able to be a part of that happening, that's very satisfying." He sees his role clearly. "I like to use a campfire image. I'm there to make sure that the fire gets lit. Everyone's attracted to the heat, but we all have to keep it going. And we do that by sitting around that fire and sharing our stories, our dreams, our goals." That's a powerful way to leave a legacy.

Grandmother

Parents have the potential to exert an enormous influence on their offspring, and when I ask parents about their legacy, they often cite their children as "their greatest legacy." Rightly or wrongly, our children may read specific expectations into this message. They may feel pressure to contribute to our legacy by going into a family business, continuing a family tradition of practising a certain occupation, achieving new heights for the family, or simply "not letting the family down." As parents, we walk a fine line between transferring our values and general-ized aspirations to our children without burdening them with constricting directives. Often, our children are highly sensitive to such signals, sometimes perceiving them when none may be intended.

For this reason, other people in the family circle have the potential to leave their mark on our children without all the drama. This has been the case for Erik and his grandmother, and it illustrates the power of a loving relationship to give a young man roots and wings.

Erik is twenty-six years old and can clearly see how his grandparents' legacy is playing out in his life. "I have grown up to be interested in the world around me," he says, "as it is today, as it was yesterday, and how it may turn out tomorrow. My grandparents have played a big part in awakening that interest. The dining table at their house has always been a place for lively discussions and thrilling tales from many corners of the world. I would hear their stories from the South African apartheid regime, Red China under Mao and the West German capital of Bonn. And, despite the fact that my grandparents' background has given them a lot of knowledge and experience, my arguments and points of view have always been treated with respect. It was always safe to join in on the discussions. Even as a child, I was encouraged to participate. To have grandparents that have taken part in the history of the world has been inspiring and empowering. It has given me a feeling of closeness to important events in our near past and is a source of pride."

Liv is eighty-one years old and remembers vividly when this grandson came into her life. "Little Erik was a beautiful baby," she says. "I fell in love with him instantly, and immediately asked his parents to please let me take him for a walk. He smiled and gurgled and was thoroughly lovable. I was fifty-five years old when he was born—young and strong enough to run with him, roll around on the floor or in the snow, lift him up and play games. I have strong memories of his first summers at the cottage. Grandfather and Erik were early risers, and Erik would sit on his grandpa's shoulders for their morning walk around the island. Erik would have a stick in his hand to ward off all the 'wild animals.' The wild animals were sheep, calmly grazing until they heard the sound of the morning patrol. After their walk, the two of them would take care of a small horse who would come to the gate to greet them and wait to be fed. After this morning ritual, we would have breakfast on the veranda. Erik loved to swim and would jump from the quay into adult arms or splash in an old bathtub we found and filled with water. We sang together, nursery rhymes, lullabies and the Beatles's "Yellow Submarine." Those first summers were the beginning of a loving relationship."

Currently, Erik is in year five of a psychology degree. He has spent summer semesters in Germany studying the language. He credits his grandmother with inspiring him to learn German and appreciates her ongoing support. "My German is pretty good," says Liv, "so I often use German in my email exchanges with Erik, and we did a German workshop together that was pretty advanced. Last year, Erik was an exchange student at a German university, and we visited him there. We had a very interesting weekend, with Erik showing us all the sights in the northeastern part of the country that was once East Germany. We always have a lot to talk about with Erik, whether an in-depth discussion about European history, or his projects at the university, including one he did interviewing eighty-year-olds about their situations. Talking to him, I can see the benefits from his psychology studies. That, in combination with his respect for his grandparents, makes for very interesting discussions. We are very lucky to have our relationship with him. And very grateful."

Erik analyzes what makes their relationship work. "For as long as I can remember, my grandparents have reached out to me as an individual," he says. "My grandmother once said that she was grateful to have grandchildren, because it gave her a new chance—a chance to do things better than she did with her children. What my grandfather said he most appreciated was that this time around, he didn't have to worry about discipline. Rather, he could focus on having positive interaction. These attitudes are a good basis on which to develop a relationship between grandchild and grandparents."

Liv has five grandchildren. I've focused on Liv's relationship with Erik because he is at the stage where he is examining himself and the role of others in his development. When I began exploring this question about Liv's impact, her four granddaughters were between the ages of fifteen and eighteen. "They are too busy being teenagers to engage in this kind of introspection," Liv explained, "but my husband and I are similarly connected to them all. We see how different they are, now that they are young women: exuberant, shy, humorous, devoted or straightforward. Every relation is unique. We bear that in mind when they are with us."

Liv says that when her grandchildren were very young, she told them to think of themselves as a house. She would illustrate her point using building blocks. "You are this house," she would say. "And one day, you will grow to be a tall, beautiful building. But first, you need to build your foundation. For that, you need work, dedication and discipline. If your foundation is solid, one day you might be a skyscraper and reach for the stars."

When I ask Liv to describe the legacy she will leave her grandchildren, here is her reply: "I trust they will remember me for as long as it makes sense to remember my values. They might remember how to build a solid skyscraper, and, very important, how to sing a song."

Mentor

Mentors and their protegés have a significant potential to influence one another in a life-changing way. The mentoring relationship might start as an informal connection inspired by proximity or shared interests. Maybe the girl next door shows an interest in learning about your career, or your friend's son asks for some pointers in your area of expertise. You might have the chance to participate in a formal mentoring program set up by your professional organization or your company to accelerate learning and open doors. In the case of Henry and Derek, whose story you'll read about next, it was a chance connection that brought them together. Their mentoring relationship bound them in a way that changed them both and sealed their legacies.

Their story began seven years ago, when Derek flew home from the UK after serving two years of a five-year prison sentence at a young offenders institution. A few weeks after his return, Derek would meet Henry, the eighty-year-old man who would become his mentor. Their relationship would give

Derek the confidence, the strategies and the contacts he needed to remake his life. And the benefits would flow both ways. Through supporting Derek, Henry would understand his own past and reach back to comfort his younger self.

Derek was nineteen years old when he returned home. "There were many questions which kept me up at night," he says. "How will I reintegrate into society? What will I do for the rest of my life? Will I be able to get a job? How will I deal with those who want to condemn me because of my past? Will I still be able to fulfill my dreams? My biggest fear was that I would never recover from my fall from grace."

Relationships like this often need a catalyst, and in this case, it was Henry's daughter, Judith. "For years, I'd heard about Derek from his grandmother," she recalls. "She was raising her two grandchildren on her own, and Derek, who was in high school then, was her pride and joy. I hadn't met him but I'd heard about his excellent grades and great work ethic. There was no place to study at home, so he'd go into town and sit in a fast-food restaurant and do his homework and prepare for exams late into the night. He was doing so well that their church group planned to support his studies after high school. But then he was arrested for smuggling drugs into the UK."

At the request of Derek's grandmother, Judith met with Derek when he came home. "I was surprised to meet this well-spoken, articulate young man, and I wanted to support him. I started inviting him to get-togethers at my home and worked with him on some writing proposals. But I really wanted

Dad to meet him. I had grown up watching Dad mentor other talented young men and I knew he had much to offer Derek. So, the next time Dad visited, I organized a party and invited Derek. After watching him in action, Dad was able to see what I saw in Derek."

Derek remembers that first gathering with Henry and Judith's friends—people who were the country's movers and shakers. "I longed to be a part of their conversations," he recalls. "People were talking about the inner workings of how things are done in the real world—politics, society, life, art. These were things I had studied and these people had actually been a part of it. I was like a sponge soaking up all this knowledge. My stratum of society was very different, so the conversations I was used to having were different, and I had never had the opportunity to meet this kind of people."

Henry remembers Derek's excitement at being exposed to this world. "There were a lot of very impressive people at the party," Henry recalls. "As people were telling their stories, Derek's jaw dropped, and he said afterwards, 'This is a whole world that I had no idea about.' I was struck by his articulateness. He'd been able to connect with people and start to talk. He had this incredible intellectual curiosity." Both Henry and Derek remember that something clicked between them. "There was a connection between us which I couldn't quite put my finger on," Derek says. "Henry has often repeated that at that meeting, he instinctively knew there was something special about me, and he wanted to help me in whatever way he could."

As they got to know one another, Henry began to see in Derek a young man with tremendous creative ability who had difficulty focusing his talents. "I knew he was a good actor; I knew he was a good dancer; I knew he wanted to write; I knew he was working on his diploma in English. It was like seeing a kid who's holding all kinds of balloons. They're all floating up there but I'm not getting a feeling of how he's going to pull them down."

But Henry knew that Derek was hindered by more than lack of focus. "I could sense his feeling that he would never succeed in the way my friends had. There was baggage there that was preventing him from getting on with what he wanted to do. Until he got to the point where he could tell his story, I felt he would be locked in. So, my mission was to pull and pull and pull." Derek remembers his frustration with Henry during that period. "I'd never told my story," Derek says. "And in Henry's persistent way, he kept asking me questions, asking hard, tough questions that I needed to answer for myself. But I was afraid. It was hard to come face-to-face with myself and what had happened. And I didn't know how to move on from there. During one of these sessions, I walked out on Henry. I couldn't take it anymore."

Henry soon found his chance to help Derek get unstuck. "I'd invited a very distinguished author and some other creative, dynamic types to join Derek and me for lunch," Henry recalls. "We were sitting on my veranda and I could see that Derek was transfixed by their stories. And suddenly I said, 'So

Derek, tell us your story.' And for the next ninety minutes, it was as though a dam had burst. He talked non-stop about his life—about growing up, about what had happened in England and why he did what he did. By the end, the listeners were in tears. I got goosebumps. It was at this point that I realized we had in our midst—what I had long suspected—a really gifted young man, capable of doing anything."

Derek looks back on the event as a bit of a set-up, but he was glad of the outcome. "I knew this author was coming to lunch to discuss my writing," he says, "and I thought it would be just me. But there were eight or ten people. I had met a couple of them a few days earlier, and I didn't even know the others—so, essentially, they were a bunch of strangers. We're all having lunch and chit-chatting and then Henry says, "Young master would like to speak now." And this was not part of the plan. My first instinct was to refuse. But I thought, 'I have to do it sometime, somehow. I can't keep living in fear of my past. I can't live with these elephants in the room because they're going to kill me.' So, I said I was ready and I started to speak. And then you couldn't stop me. I didn't make eye contact with anyone because I was ashamed. I expected them to judge and condemn me because I'd grown to expect that for someone with a past like mine. But when I finished, I raised my head and saw that almost everyone was in tears. And then they commended me for my courage and for being able to endure that experience—and not only to endure it but to be able to speak of it and to be able to pull myself up. They said things like, 'You haven't kept yourself down.' 'You're doing all right for yourself, man.' 'Give yourself some credit for not staying down.' So as much as I had avoided it, I believe speaking about my experience was necessary. I had to cross that barrier. It gave me the motivation to move on.

"After that, Henry and I kind of planned the way forward as to where my skills were most suited and where I needed help and assistance. And I think we kind of merged his ideas and my ideas and my dreams to find something of a direction—something that would help me lead a dignified life, a life worth living."

Throughout the mentoring process, Henry has given Derek practical life strategies and techniques, along with personal connections. And he keeps the pressure on. "One of the qualities I really appreciate about Henry, though it also annoys me," Derek says, "is that he continually pushes me to exceed my own expectations and face my fears. His nudging, which can be uncomfortable, is constant and I know that ultimately, his relentlessness is helpful. He refuses to give up on me, even when I give up on myself."

Henry says this "push and push back" sets up a creative tension that is the foundation of his mentoring approach. Derek agrees. "Our relationship is multi-faceted, and not without its struggles," he says. "Many times, Henry and I don't see eye to eye and sometimes we agree to disagree. I appreciate that in those instances, he chooses to respect my opinions. He does not enforce his will on me despite the fact that he has over eighty years of experience under his belt. Instead, he finds creative ways to teach me."

Judith can see the results of her dad's approach. "Derek had to realize he had everything he needed to succeed except for belief in himself," she says. "The experiences he's had with Dad have given him confidence. He saw that he could hold his own in any setting and be accepted as an equal based on the strength of his intelligence, talent and wonderful personality. He understands that he is as worthy of opportunities as anyone else. He knows he holds the key to his own success."

When Henry reflects on the mentoring process, he realizes that what was happening to him was as important as what Derek was going through. "I had spent my entire life packaging away things that I didn't want to deal with—my own growing up and the loneliness I felt, and the rejection," he says. "Derek pushed me into looking at myself and it was an incredible, liberating experience."

Henry and Derek call their relationship their "extraordinary 80/20 journey," referring to their age difference, and I ask Judith what she thinks is the key to its success. She says her father has become the positive male role model Derek never had. "Prior to this," she says, "the only older male figures in his life were his and his sister's absent fathers, and his uncles. And it was the uncles who brought him into the drug world and coerced him into smuggling drugs into the UK. So, to have an older male figure like Dad take an interest in him in a meaningful way must have meant the world to him. I think Dad's greatest gift to Derek was never giving up on him."

The cement that holds the 80/20 relationship together is their love for one another. A few months ago, Derek sent a thank you note to Henry. "I am grateful for you and the wisdom that you've shared with me," he wrote. "I am grateful that you have never given up on me. I am grateful for your kindness and generosity. I am grateful for your love. This is just a gentle reminder that I thank God that you are a part of my life, and I love ya ole fella. I love ya very much." Henry replied, "You have done as much for me as you say I have done for you. Ours is a story of love and understanding and respect for each other, which, if others followed, would make this world a better place."

Since Derek's return from the UK, he has won awards for his acting and has worked as a dancer, singer and choreographer. He has written a play based on his time in prison and is writing a memoir about his experiences. When I ask him about his goals for the future, he focuses on mentoring. "I want to lead, to inspire people and help them reach their best and highest potential, in whatever way I can. I am an artist, so perhaps it's through my art. At the end of the day, titles and money go. What is left is the memory and the impact you've had on others. I hope to continue a legacy of hope for those who need to be encouraged and inspired."

Philosopher King

Some people leave their legacy by making a deep and meaningful connection with countless people they encounter every day. This was the case for Peter Verin, who was living on the streets of Victoria, BC, in 2017 when he died just short of his seventy-second birthday. Verin collected recyclables in shopping carts, slept where he could find shelter, and was always ready to stop for a philosophical discussion. People say he would have been taken aback to find that his life had been memorialized with a granite bench bearing the title "Our Philosopher King." The carved tribute reads: "You touched all our hearts. We were blessed to know you."

Many members of Verin's broad and diverse social network found out about one another after his death. According to the *Times Colonist*, the crowd that showed up at his memorial service included "a retired UVic vice-president, students, librarians, Saanich police officers, paramedics, baristas, grocery clerks, city workers, politicians, hairdressers and several homeless people."[1] When a couple of these friends launched a fundraising effort to create some permanent commemoration for Verin, they never imagined they would raise $3,400. They had enough money for the bench, a plaque and some left over to be donated to organizations that help homeless people.

Technically, Verin was homeless, but this was not how he saw himself. David Turner, a retired University of Victoria professor, says that from Verin's point of view, "he was living a particular free-spirit lifestyle." Turner first met Verin in the early

1970s when Verin was roaming the university campus, pulling textbooks from garbage bins and chatting up students at the library. "He was kind of a live-in professor," says Turner.[2] It was true that Verin had some academic training—he had studied philosophy in his twenties at McGill University—but he called himself a "professional salvager," recycling things others threw away in an effort to mediate the carelessness of our wasteful society.

Verin's random encounters delighted and affected people, as we can see in the following Facebook posting from someone who ran across him in 2014: "To the homeless man named Peter who is always around Quadra/Mckenzie area, shout out to you for being one of the most humble and intelligent people I've ever talked to! Today at the bottle depot we offered you $10 and the only thing you'd accept was our bottles because you said it made you feel better working for your money. You're so friendly and I hear you're good at recommending books to people! If anyone sees a shorter and older man with a bit of a hunchback around the area I'm sure he'd appreciate your bottles!"[3]

Verin spent his evenings at the local library reading magazines, using the computers and listening to podcasts. The librarian Delia Filipescu said that Verin gave her a different perspective about people living on the streets. "He had a knowledge I never expected. I was the librarian but he was answering the questions. Wherever you are, Peter, we are missing you," she said.[4]

Greg Pratt, editor of *Nexus*, Camosun College's student

newspaper, remembers running into Verin from the time he was a kid, and his shopping cart was always full of salvaged stuff, including lots of reading material. "He was always happy to stop and talk philosophy or some other academic matter, and he always wanted to learn what the other person had to say." Pratt wrote the following tribute in his *Nexus* memorial to Verin: "His charming demeanour and encyclopedic knowledge will be missed; the lesson he leaves behind about living life on your own terms will not be forgotten."[5]

Our life story is part of our legacy, and the next chapter looks at how we record that story and the way we craft our version of the truth. Let's consider the stories you've just read. In the case of those who are deceased, I summarized their lives from their biographies and personal writings, which are a matter of public record. When it comes to the living, either their stories have received media attention or I interviewed them and formed their stories from their accounts of their lives. If we don't figure out a way to capture our own lives, we're missing an opportunity to put our imprint in the history books. Disappearing without a trace may not be the worst outcome. As you'll read in the next chapter, it may be more troubling if someone else writes our story.

Who Tells Our Story

One way to try and manage our legacy is to take control of our own narrative. Rather than leave the details of our future persona to chance, we can record our story, our way. The author Dave Eggers writes in *The Autobiographer's Handbook* that we have a duty to write ourselves into existence. "You should write your story because you will someday die, and without your story on paper, most of it will be forgotten." Writing our memoir not only preserves our story, Eggers says, but it is also a therapeutic process. "To delve, for a year or years, into your past, with an eye for detail and organization—to look for patterns and signals in your own life and to control its narrative ... What could be more healing than that?"[1]

Augie Merasty was living on the streets of Prince Albert, Saskatchewan, and if he hadn't written his memoir, his story would likely have been forgotten. His book, *The Education of Augie Merasty*, was published in 2015, when he was eighty-five years old, and describes the abuse he suffered as a Cree boy in a residential school. He spent about a decade collaborating on the book with the author David Carpenter, and it was Carpenter who facilitated its publication. The book was a national bestseller and a nominee for several awards. Merasty wrote, "I sincerely hope that what I have related here will have some impact so all that has happened in our school, and other schools in all parts of Canada—the abuse and terror in the lives of Indian children—does not occur ever again."[2] Merasty died at age eighty-seven, and his words have left a powerful legacy that shines a light on the dark passages of our history.

While Merasty wrote his story to document a wrong, Colin Henthorne wrote his to rescue his good name. Henthorne was the captain of the BC ferry *Queen of the North*, which sank in 2006 after running off course and striking an underwater ledge near remote Gil Island, BC. The ship sank in just over an hour. One hundred and one people were on board. All were evacuated successfully with the exception of two people who went missing and were subsequently declared deceased. In 2016, Henthorne published *The Queen of the North Disaster: The Captain's Story* in order to get his version of events on the public record. Henthorne's book is a detailed account of both the ship's sinking and the aftermath and includes a timed chronology of the night of the accident, the ship's layout and specifications, and an in-depth description of the ship's steering equipment.

Henthorne, who was off watch and asleep at the time of the incident, was never charged with wrongdoing in the sinking. The BC Provincial Court charged Karl Lilgert, the crew member who was responsible for steering the ferry at the time of the accident, with criminal negligence causing death. In 2013,

Lilgert was found guilty and sentenced to four years in prison. Henthorne's book includes this man's apology statement.

Henthorne was subsequently fired by BC Ferries. He says it was because he raised the issue of safety standards; the company said it was because of his behaviour during their internal investigation. Henthorne says it took him more than six years to recover his career, and the recovery has not been a full one.

Henthorne notes in his book that the Justice Institute of British Columbia recognized the crew of the *Queen of the North* with a Heroes and Rescue Award in 2008, acknowledging the challenges they faced in evacuating the passengers into life rafts in the pitch black in the remote location as the ship was rapidly sinking.[3]

A mariner who is familiar with the waters where the ship went down said his mind was changed by reading Henthorne's book. "At the time of the sinking, there was a lot of negative media coverage about Henthorne's role, but after reading his version of events, I find it hard to fault his actions. There is a lot of blame to go around when a tragedy like this occurs, and I'm glad he documented the fuller picture." Henthorne introduces his book with a quote from Joseph Conrad: "You can't, in sound morals, condemn a man for taking care of his own integrity. It is his clear duty."

Making a record of our lives allows us to explain things from our perspective and gives others insight into what we were thinking and why we did what we did. We may assume that others understand our motivation for our actions or see the reasoning behind our behaviour, but we may be overly optimistic. One of my interviewees decided it was time to tell her own story when she realized her teenage sons were making unfounded and unfair assumptions about her life choices. "Recently, I was having dinner with my boys and they started talking about their childhood. It was a shock for me to realize that they had no understanding of why I had worked as hard as I did when they were young. They seemed to think I preferred working to any other possible activity, including being with them. At first, I was angry with them and then I realized it was my own fault. I'd never talked about our financial struggles during that period and my need to establish my career. So, how would they have known? That got me thinking about all the other things they may not know about me, and I decided it's time to write it down."

Erik is the young man who describes the positive role his grandparents play in his life in the previous chapter. A couple of years ago, Erik asked his grandparents to write down the stories of their lives. When I interviewed his grandmother Liv, she told me about Erik's request and admitted she hadn't gotten around to tackling the project. After our discussion, she decided to make writing her memoir a priority. The result is *My Story: 1936–1998*, a fifty-page book with text and full-colour photos that detail her life. Liv wrote the memoir herself and selected the photos, and then worked with a computer designer to create a digital document for easy reproduction.

"It will be a Christmas present for our sons and our grand-children," she says, "as well as for my two brothers. I've written a preface in which I tell the story of how this piece of writing came about. I conclude by saying how we love all five of our grandchildren dearly. In the memoir, I present a version of myself which I hope will inspire them. I had to balance between truth and honesty, and the impetus to be entertaining. Of course, there are some elephants in the room. We all have some, but we do not parade them! My message to my grand-children is: 'The more you know and understand, the more interesting your life will be.' And now my husband says he's going to write his own story—just to set the record straight!"

Liv is now trying to inspire her friends to write their mem-oirs as a gift for their grandchildren. "One friend told me she had already written her story," Liv says, "but some of the family members mentioned in it were not pleased with her account. Another friend said she had no wish to recapitulate her life; it had been too difficult. And the third said her recollection of her past was incomplete, and her writing skills were not good enough to turn her story into an interesting piece of reading." Liv's advice is to focus on your readers and assume they will appreciate getting to know you better. "Sprinkle your story with important dates and happenings from the times in which your life took place," she says. "Try to be funny, or emotional—or both."

I would add that it's important to tackle this task when you have the memory, the energy and the research skills to pull it off. It helps to write things down periodically to provide an ongoing record so you don't have to retrieve it all from memory. Over the years, my brothers and I received envelopes in the mail from my father containing brief family history essays. These documents were written in response to a variety of circumstances. When my husband and I planned a monumental road trip from Ontario to the Pacific Ocean, Dad wrote a detailed account of my grandparents' time in the West and suggested we track down some relatives en route. A question from a grandson who was working on a school project for Remembrance Day inspired a chronology of the many battles our ancestors had participated in over the centuries. Dad's trip to the East Coast to arrange for the burial of his parents' ashes spurred a fascinating history of our family's shipbuilding days. Pulling together this extensive amount of information would have been beyond his capacity later in life, and these family stories would probably have been buried with him.

Why Do Family Stories Matter?

Author and journalist Bruce Feiler has written about the role of family stories in moulding a happy family and says that children who have the most self-confidence have a strong "intergenerational self." "They know they belong to something bigger than themselves," he writes. Feiler cites the research of Dr. Marshall Duke and Dr. Robyn Fivush, who developed the "Do You Know?" scale, a set of twenty questions that measures how well children know their family history. Questions include: "Do you know an illness or something terrible that happened in your family?" "Do you know the story of your birth?" "Do you know where your grandparents grew up?" Their research concluded that this scale was their best single predictor of a child's emotional health and happiness. The more the child knew about his family's history, the stronger his sense of control over his life, the higher his self-esteem and the more successfully he believed his family functioned.[4]

Marjorie's father never told her the truth about her heritage, and she regrets deeply having been denied this connection with her roots. "One of the most important legacies we get from our parents is their cultural or societal legacy," she says. "I was thirty-five years old and the mother of two children before I learned my father was Jewish." Her parents had been married in a Catholic ceremony—she'd seen the photos. And she and her siblings had been baptized in a long white dress that came from her father's family. As she was growing up, her family life had been centred on the parish church. Marjorie remembers being told that her father had converted to Catholicism and that before that he had been "nothing." It was her father's sister who eventually admitted under questioning that their family was Jewish, but she said they "never practised."

"Judaism happens to be a particularly rich legacy— historically, culturally, ethically," Marjorie says. "Not knowing what shaped my father, nor what he rejected in terms of values and history, deprived me of something that could have been an important part of me. Learning about it later in life is not the same thing." Marjorie recognizes now that her father instilled in his children the most important of Jewish values. "We learned the primacy of family, education and altruism," she says. "We learned the importance of 'trying to mend a broken world,' as the Jews say. But figuring this out after the fact is a poor second best compared to a childhood imbued with this legacy. Not to mention the many interesting and simpatico relatives that my father—for a reason that still escapes us—kept us from knowing."

When my daughter was fourteen years old, we embarked on a three-generation project, working with my aunt to tell the story of my mother's side of the family. My aunt was the sole repository of my maternal history, and once she reached her eighties, I realized we needed to capture her storehouse of memories while we were still able. We worked out a process whereby she would write her stories in longhand, and I would type them up for her review and edit. My daughter would sift through family photos with her for inclusion in her family history. Armed with this background, we took a family trip to Scotland in search of the people and places my aunt had described, and visited our clan's ancestral home and its chief. We combined a report of this trip with my aunt's research to form a narrative of family history.

As my aunt reached the end of her life, it gave her great pleasure to see the family's heritage taken seriously, and it relieved her greatly that the past wouldn't die with her. The process connected us with the maternal side of my family, and introduced me, my husband and our daughters to some fascinating personal history. Our clan was led by a female chieftain for half a century and fought under the clan motto *Fortis et Fidus* (Strong and Faithful). Armed with this vivid ancestry, I have been shameless in embellishing the tales of our Highland legacy for my daughters and painting them as descendants of warrior women.

But what about families that don't want to share all of their history with their children? In my interviews, people sometimes referred to the "skeletons in the closet," and some of these secrets may not be appropriate for young ears. Clinical psychologist Dr. Robert Brooks agrees that some stories are not suitable for youngsters but finds that children may know more than we think they do. "While most, if not all, families have skeletons in the closet, I have been impressed by how many children have a sense of these skeletons even though their parents are not aware that their children possess this knowledge," he wrote. I would add that given the vivid imagination of children, in some cases the crimes they create to fill the gap of information could be more lurid than the reality.

Brooks is on the faculty of Harvard Medical School, and his work with families focuses on nurturing children's resilience, self-esteem and motivation. He finds that sharing family histories with our children creates a feeling of connectedness and an "intergenerational self." These vehicles can serve as "the scaffolding for adding meaning to the life of each family member." Brooks emphasizes that even family histories that are filled with distrust, anger and trauma can be used as learning tools. "Telling children about these unpleasant events at the appropriate time can be used to teach them about the importance of such qualities as resilience, forgiveness, responsibility, and compassion."[5]

Where Do We Start?

If you'd like to kick-start a family history project, one source for tools and advice is NPR's StoryCorps, whose mission is to record, preserve and share the stories of Americans. Their website has a list of questions that provide stimulating discussion about legacy, starting with "How would you like to be remembered?" The organization suggests the questions could be used during Thanksgiving by a student interviewing an elder, or by someone looking to spark lively conversation around their "Friendsgiving" table. History teachers are asked to encourage their students to record interviews with their families using the StoryCorps app. The app helps users select questions, and then record and upload their interviews to the StoryCorps archive in the American Folklife Center at the Library of Congress.[6] The Government of Canada has a website that gathers together a variety of resources to help you access genealogical records and start your family history research.[7]

When Abby turned seventy, she began writing about her eventful life in order to record the family history for her children. She wanted some support with the process and decided to take a course on memoir writing offered by the continuing studies program at her local university. Abby found the course provided her with the insights she needed, and she particularly appreciated that her fellow students were all ages. "The instructor stressed that it's good to record your life at any stage," she says. "You don't need to wait until the end to start this process. In fact, the earlier you begin recording the better, because the basis of memoir writing is learning how to mine our memories for good stories."

After the course ended, Abby and three other students decided to continue meeting as a memoir group. "Our little group ranges in age from me in my seventies to the youngest, who's in her forties," she says. "We've been meeting for over a year. We try and meet monthly, and for each meeting, we have an assignment to write an essay of about six pages. We send our essays to one another in advance and come to the meeting prepared with our comments and suggestions. Over the course of the evening, we discuss each person's essay one by one. Our comments are wide-ranging. We might suggest something structural, including word choices or questions of grammar. Or we might ask for clarification of something that isn't clear, or request more information."

The members of the group have different goals. "I'm going to compile my essays, add photos and other visual memorabilia and produce a memoir for my family," Abby says. "One member of the group is writing with an eye to publication. Another had a colourful career in politics, and she had been hoping to adapt the memoir she's working on and produce a work of fiction, but this is proving difficult. The last member, like me, is writing a memoir for her family."

Periodically, Abby sends her essays to her children and asks them for comments. They may ask for more information or pose questions that she then uses to expand the essay. But Abby's process hasn't worked for everyone. "Another member is no longer circulating her essays to her family," Abby says. "After her son queried, 'Have you never heard of a comma?' she decided to keep her work to herself. She'll leave her memoir in a box for her family to find."

In addition to circulating her work to her family, Abby is using a similar process to incorporate other perspectives. "Sometimes, I send my writing out to other people with a request for them to add their information," she says. "For example, I was in a car accident and I sent my essay out to the other people in the accident and asked them to add their point of view. Also, I had some surgery done recently and have struggled with the aftermath, so I decided to write an essay about my experience. When I told my surgeon that I was going to write an essay about the process, he asked to have a copy. He said he really wanted to know more about the patient perspective. My physiotherapist made the same request. If they have comments to make, I would welcome their input."

Abby has found the process to be enriching, both for herself and for her family. "Thanks to the memoir writing, my children know a lot more about me, and I know a lot more about myself," she says. "And I've really enjoyed getting to know the members of my memoir group in this intimate way."

Memoirs take all forms, from simple stapled printed pages to video biographies complete with music, titles and special effects. Online tools have made it easier to produce compelling products, but if you're feeling overwhelmed, you might benefit from involving a personal historian. To get your written memories into a readable form, you can hire a professional editor. One source for finding your collaborator is the Editors' Association of Canada.[8] Their website has an online directory of over four hundred editors across the country and offers suggestions on how to get started, including getting a cost estimate. Wilfrid Laurier University has a Life Writing series and they will publish memoirs that are well written and have a link to Canadian history. One of the women I interviewed for my book *You Could Live a Long Time: Are You Ready?* had her autobiography published under this program. In her case, the book was first self-published and then submitted for consideration to Life Writing. Wilfrid Laurier University Press published their own version of her memoir, focusing only on the Canadian portion of her story.

On one level, the digital world has made it simple to record our family history. After all, we have thousands of images and dozens of videos from every important event and many unimportant ones. But digital file folders can be just as meaningless as the bags of old black and white photos that families pass along from generation to generation for basement storage. If we don't know what we're looking at, or who these people are, or what they're doing, it's a frustrating exercise. One solution is to create a narrative and turn our history into a story where people are identified and timelines explained. The choice of medium is wide, including video, family website, digital book and audio, but the crucial issue has remained unchanged over the centuries: it takes time and foresight to turn your family history into something that people in the future are going to want to watch, listen to or read.

Then there's technological change to consider. I'm really sorry our family has lost its ability to easily view our Super 8 film footage and our Beta videotapes. It would still be feasible for us to listen to our audiotapes or flip through our 35 milli-metre slides if our players and projectors weren't broken and unlikely to be repaired. There are companies that will do dig-ital conversions and I've been meaning to get that organized.[9] Maybe someday I will. But if I really want to guarantee that my story will be adaptable to future upgrades for generations to come, maybe I should write a play, choreograph a dance or compose a song—and print a hard copy of the work.

If you want to control your own narrative and tell your story your way, it's best to write down what you want remem-bered about you and destroy any material you want spared from future scrutiny. The next best bet is to place your trust in the executor of your will and assign them the task of doc-ument destruction or protection. The story of American poet

Sylvia Plath illustrates what can happen if you abdicate responsibility for making the decision and just let the chips fall where they may.

Sylvia Plath

Sylvia Plath died by suicide at age thirty, leaving behind two very young children and no will. She had been married to poet Ted Hughes for six years; after he initiated an affair with another woman, he moved out. Four months later, Plath, who had been struggling with mental health issues, took her own life. Because she died without a will, Hughes inherited her possessions, including her unpublished manuscripts. He was in the compromised position of being both Plath's literary editor and a character in her writing, and was accused of destroying and losing Plath's journals and trying to silence her voice.

By the time of Plath's death in 1963, her work had gained a foothold. Her writing had appeared in many magazines in the US and the UK, and a collection of her poetry had been published. But it was her semi-autobiographical novel, *The Bell Jar*, that was to become a publishing sensation and a clarion call to feminists. Plath had received shock treatment for clinical depression as a college student and, in the book, she reimagines this experience through the protagonist, Esther Greenwood. Esther's mental illness is portrayed as the inevitable outcome of the restricted role placed on women in the 1950s and was read as a powerful social critique. Prior to Plath's death, the book was published in the UK under a pseudonym. In 1971, when the book was released in the US under Plath's real name, it became a commercial success, and remained on the *New York Times* bestseller list for six months.

Hughes's inheritance included copyright to all Plath's published and unpublished work, which encompassed poetry, fiction, letters and journals. When it came to getting Plath's work published, Hughes admired her writing and had a financial interest in its success, but examples abound of the conflict of interest posed by his role as her editor. When Plath died, she had left on her desk a manuscript of forty-one poems titled *Ariel*. The version of *Ariel* published in 1965, edited by Hughes, was a very different book. Hughes ignored the narrative arc Plath had established for the manuscript by reshuffling poems, omitting some and adding others. And he provided no editorial notes acknowledging his changes. Plath's biographer Paul Alexander quotes Hughes as saying he wanted to excise some of Plath's "more personally aggressive" poems.[10] When Hughes was severely criticized for these omissions, he defended himself by saying his actions were based on "concern for certain people" at whom certain poems were "aimed too nakedly." Diane Middlebrook, author of *Her Husband: Ted Hughes and Sylvia Plath—A Marriage*, writes, "Most of these poems had to do with their marriage and were aimed at him, so unsympathetic commentators tended to regard the omissions as a cover-up."[11]

In 1966, Hughes assigned his sister, Olwyn Hughes, the role of literary agent for Plath's estate. Middlebrook wrote, "It appeared to outsiders that Hughes was using his sister to protect himself from questions and had appointed Olwyn to censor rather than broker the discussion of Plath's work."[12] Having Olwyn Hughes involved in her estate is unlikely to have pleased Plath. The last time she saw Olwyn was at a Hughes family gathering, when they had a significant altercation. Plath wrote to her mother that Olwyn had called her "intolerant, selfish, inhospitable, and immature—words she flung at her out of hatred."[13] Plath declared that she would never again stay in the same house with Olwyn.

Hughes is said to have been careless with his responsibilities as custodian of Plath's work, often leaving her material out in the open. Some of Plath's manuscripts were stolen by Hughes's partner to create a nest egg for the support of the daughter she had with Hughes. She turned them over to her sister, and according to the sister, she took "quite a lot." The sister later returned the material to Hughes.[14] The losses under Hughes's watch included the deliberate destruction of Plath's last journal, which Hughes did not want her children to read. Middlebrook wrote that a critic reprimanded Hughes, "comparing him to the literary executors of Lord Byron's estate who shredded his papers. Hughes defended his action not as a literary executor, but as a father—as if burning the pages was the only way to keep them out of the hands of the children."[15]

Hughes's actions were publicly decried. In the UK, for example, the poet and author A. Alvarez, who had described Plath as "the most gifted woman poet of her time," published a critique of Hughes's editorial approach in the *Observer*, in which he questioned Hughes's censorship.[16] American novelist and poet Erica Jong criticized Hughes for pruning Sylvia's work when he was "the very man who pruned her life."[17]

In 1982, Plath's *Collected Poems* received the Pulitzer Prize. Her work has been the focus of countless studies and critical essays, and her dedicated fan base buys almost anything she wrote. So, when it came to her literary life, Plath's legacy was secure. But it appeared that Plath's take on her own life would remain censored. This changed in 2017 with the publication of *The Letters of Sylvia Plath: Volume 1: 1940–1956*, which released her unedited voice.[18] The correspondence included letters to some 120 people, including family, friends, contemporaries and colleagues—and most of the letters had never been seen. A second volume will continue this publication of Plath's unfiltered thoughts. Through the monumental gathering of this scattered collection, the editors have given Plath as close to an autobiography as she'll ever get.

By leaving no will, Plath both gave up her agency and placed Hughes in an untenable position. He was caught in the conflicting roles of literary flame-keeper, concerned father, impugned partner and assiduous editor. In the final analysis, Hughes's positive contribution to Plath's legacy, although flawed, requires acknowledgement. He was successful in keeping Plath's work in the public eye and further contributed to her memory through his own writing. His collection of poems *Birthday Letters*, which was published around the time of his death in 1998, addressed his relationship with Plath. Middlebrook says this writing continued the theme of everything Hughes published after her death: "how marriages fail, or how men fail in marriage."[19]

Whom would Plath have preferred to control her legacy? We'll never know—and therein lies the problem. If we think that Plath's issues apply only to writers, and famous ones at that, we need to remind ourselves that someone is going to go through our personal effects after our death and decide what to preserve as part of our legacy. Forearmed with Plath's example, we need to ensure we have a sympathetic sorter who will act in the best interests of our afterlife. What should give us pause is imagining this happening tomorrow rather than decades from now, when we assume we'll have tackled this task ourselves.

Censoring Ourselves

Sylvia Plath's legacy was pruned and packaged to fit other agendas. One of the issues we face is how much we should censor ourselves. To what extent do we clean up our own image and manage our own stories? Writing our memoirs is one way of portraying our lives as we wish them to be seen. As Liv earlier described the process: "Of course there are some elephants in the room. We all have some, but we do not parade them!" But what about our diaries or journals, or the letters in our possession? While we're alive, we may not be prepared to part with this material, but do we want it circulating after we're gone? Do we put the items of concern in a file labelled "Destroy without reading upon my death," or do we parade our elephants for history to see?

I recently found a stack of letters my husband and I had sent to one another over the early years of our relationship and immediately decided they were too personal for public exposure and should be destroyed. But then a friend who had lost her husband told me how comforting it was to reread their correspondence. And then I heard Helen's story, which you'll read in more detail later. Helen's parents were killed in a car accident, and when the family gathered for a wake, they brought out their parents' old love letters and read them aloud, and laughed until the tears ran down their cheeks. So, that adds another dimension. Maybe I should hang on to our letters to provide this kind of solace—or entertainment. It's hard to decide what to do with them. But, as we know, not taking action is actually a decision—so there they stay.

Another approach is to always write your correspondence with an eye to your legacy. This was the approach of the Czech-born, German-speaking writer Rainer Maria Rilke and the reason we have his *Letters to a Young Poet*, one of the most beloved books of the twentieth century. The young poet in question was aspiring nineteen-year-old Franz Xaver Kappus, who had written to twenty-seven-year-old Rilke to ask for a critique of his poetry. It was 1903, and Rilke had just moved to Paris to write a book about the sculptor Auguste Rodin. Over the next five years, they exchanged some twenty letters, and Rilke's advice to Kappus is Rodin's wisdom as much as Rilke's own.

Rilke's letters are compelling because he treated their writing as part of his poetic practice. His biographer Rachel

Corbett wrote that Rilke "took such care in composing his correspondence—he would sooner rewrite an entire page of script than mar its surface with a crossed-out word—that he gave his publisher permission to posthumously release it."[20] Rilke died in 1926, and a collection of ten of his letters to Kappus was published in 1929 as *Letters to a Young Poet*. Kappus was right when he predicted that the letters would stir the hearts of other "growing and evolving spirits of today and tomorrow."[21] Rilke's advice to Kappus has become part of contemporary culture and is shared at weddings and graduations in reflections such as "Perhaps everything that frightens us is, in its deepest essence, something helpless that wants our love" and "I hold this to be the highest task of a bond between two people: that each should stand guard over the solitude of the other."

What about our diaries and journals? Unfiltered private musings can be explosive devices that destroy not just our own legacy but others', or they can reveal aspects of ourselves that we don't mind having unveiled—after we're gone. L. M. Montgomery, best known for her series of novels beginning with *Anne of Green Gables*, deliberately left the spicy bits in her journals so her family could see her as she wished to be seen. In a review of Montgomery's journals, author and academic Carole Gerson wrote, "Despite her conservative demeanor, she [Montgomery] included a frank account of her youthful love affairs because she wanted her unborn descendants to know that their greying grandmother was once 'young and brown-tressed . . . and was called a flirt by my enemies.'" Gerson says the journals provide a record of feelings and concerns that were not communicated through any of Montgomery's public selves. [22]

The poet Rumi is said to have taken great comfort from his father's private writings, and carried pages around with him, tucked into the inner sleeve pocket of his robe. In *Rumi's Secret*, Brad Gooch explains that Rumi's father, Baha Valad, was outwardly strict and emphasized the wages of sin. But his private journal was filled with intimate meditations on divine love expressed in passionate language. Gooch says the journal was Baha Valad's "most durable gift to his son" and "allowed Rumi to hear the voice of his dear father once again, filling him with warmth and purpose, and informing his ideas about love and God."[23]

I had heard that the revered West Coast artist and writer Emily Carr stoked bonfires with her rejected artwork and writings and seemed to have been very much in control of her own legacy. But then I read that Carr's private journals had been published, exposing her unedited musings. I tried to understand why these journals hadn't been destroyed and what we can learn from that story.

Emily Carr

Emily Carr left a monumental legacy of art and published books, including an autobiography, all of which were released into the world with her stamp of approval. But while she was continually making decisions about what to keep and what to discard, with an eye to posterity, her private journals seemed to have escaped her scrutiny.

Carr died in 1945 at age seventy-three and her autobiography, *Growing Pains*, was published a year after her death. Her biographer Maria Tippett wrote that the book "owed more to literary art than to the faithfulness of her recollections." Carr told her story her way by embroidering incidents and inventing dialogue to create a series of short sketches. She worried the memoir might "shock or distress" her relatives and prohibited its publication during her lifetime. Indeed, her sister Alice wrote that her recollection of their childhood was different from that portrayed in Carr's journals. "I know it is a wonderful piece of literature, but to me the things she says in it are very hurtful, some parts I love and read over and over, other parts I skip."[24]

In addition to crafting her autobiography, Carr culled her art and her personal papers with a nod to her legacy. Each time she moved, she cleaned house and burned paintings, letters and stories. After one such cleanup, she wrote, "The junk has gone. The auction discards have gone. One big bonfire has blazed a thousand memories into oblivion and another waits for the match."[25] She explained her decision to burn a pile of old sketches: "They are not good or big enough to whip up any imagination in others."[26]

Carr was also sensitive about the letters others had sent to her, including those from Lawren Harris, the renowned artist and member of the Group of Seven. She met Harris in 1927 and they corresponded for many years. He provided her with much-needed advice and support when she was struggling to find her artistic path. Harris knew Carr suffered from depression and feelings of isolation, and he encouraged her to persevere. "When we enter the stream of creative life—then we are on our own—have to find self reliance—achieve conviction— learn to accept—and begin to see a supreme logic behind the inner struggle," he wrote to her.[27] Carr kept many of her letters from Harris but decided to burn a few she thought were too personal.[28]

Toward the end of her life, Carr carefully sorted through the last of her belongings with her friend Carol Pearson. In her book, *Emily Carr As I Knew Her*, Pearson wrote that she sat beside Carr's bed as they went through drawers and boxes for what seemed to her like hours. They sorted bundles of letters, packing some in boxes and burning others. Carr's last request was that Pearson bury some boxes of small personal treasures in Beacon Hill Park near her home in Victoria, BC. "These things would be of no value to anyone else, but they are a part of me, my past. I cannot bring myself to burn them. Take them, Child, out into the woods, and bury them for me, a box at a time, where they will rest with the trees, through the years. My spirit will rest with them."[29] The buried items included a pair of men's large, old gold cufflinks, small worn books of poetry, bits of jewellery, mostly broken, small worn dog collars, faded pictures and a little mesh purse.

Pearson said that Carr's preparation for death included making her own burial shroud, and she asked Pearson to lay it away in her bottom drawer. Pearson explained this action by saying that Carr was always thinking about other people's feelings. "She did not wish her sister, who was blind, to have extra trouble when the end came."[30]

Carr made Ira Dilworth her literary executor and appointed him and Lawren Harris as trustees of the Emily Carr Trust. Eighty pictures were to be selected as the Emily Carr Picture Collection, with forty-five to be put in the trust and thirty-five to be sold to maintain it. Carr, Harris and Dilworth chose the forty-five paintings, and they were given to the Vancouver Art Gallery on permanent loan. One of the provisions in Carr's will was to set up a scholarship fund "to enable art students residing in British Columbia to study art at some art school or art schools to be selected by the Trustees." Tippett wrote that just before Carr died, she experienced a measure of contentment from knowing that her affairs were settled, combined with some personal reconciliations she had made. And to add to Carr's happiness, a few days before her death, she was elated to learn that the University of British Columbia was going to confer on her the degree of Doctor of Letters.[31]

Given Carr's thorough legacy planning, it is surprising that she seemed to have left the matter of her journals up in the air. Carr treated her journals both as a confessional and as a way of working out her thinking, and reading them is an intimate experience. We have access to the journals because Dilworth, her literary executor, began transcribing them from twenty notebooks she had entrusted to him. After Dilworth's death, the process was completed through the authority of one of his heirs. In 1966, the first edition of the journals, titled

Hundreds and Thousands: The Journals of Emily Carr, was published by Clarke, Irwin & Company.

Art historian Gerta Moray, who wrote the introduction to a 2006 edition of the journals, concludes it is unlikely Carr would have written so frankly if she had thought her journals would be published. She surmises that Carr "would have felt horrified to see her most naked thoughts on a printed page."[32] After all, when Carr found out that Lawren Harris had shown some of her letters to others, she wrote in her journal, "I could not write my innermost thoughts if *anybody* was to read them."[33] The notebooks were written over a period of fifteen years, and Carr's journaling practice was irregular. Moray emphasizes that the journals are selective and spontaneous, and should not be confused with autobiography or memoirs.

While Carr may not have intended this material for public viewing, there is no evidence that she made such a direction explicit. And she did not destroy these notebooks, unlike other material she wanted removed from the spotlight. Her journals contain some insight into her thinking on this matter. At one point after she had just finished destroying and burning stories, papers and letters, Carr wrote that she couldn't bear to get rid of everything—not yet. "You forget how much some of the friends out of the past loved you till you read again some loving letters." However, "if you knew *when* you were going out you'd destroy all."[34] Maybe the journals missed her deadline.

Whether deliberately or inadvertently, by allowing us to read her journals, Carr has allowed us into her heart and soul to ride the peaks and valleys of her artistic life. Through her raw words, we feel her struggles with poverty, depression and low self-esteem, and share her frustration when she couldn't get her vision down on paper, or when she felt unappreciated by her fellow artists, her community and her family.

We also get to share her victories. One of her most compelling achievements was the necessary breaking free from her mentor Lawren Harris. Initially, Carr positions Harris and the rest of the Group of Seven as severe taskmasters who "will be dissatisfied when they see my work."[35] Then the relationship passes to the stage of modest encouragement: "Jackson and Lismer both felt that though my knowledge was poor, I had got the spirit of the country and the people more than the others who had been there."[36] At last, the student reaches the point where she must break away from the teacher and strike out on her own: "Now they [the criticisms and ideals of the East] are torn away and I stand *alone* on my own perfectly good feet. Now I take my own soul as my critic."[37]

Carr's story is an impetus for us to tackle the difficult task of dealing with our most intimate and revealing records. I'm grateful that Carr's published journals are now in my hands, but she may not have been so pleased.

Curating Our Digital Selves

So far, these discussions about controlling our legacy have focused on letters, journals, writings, paintings—all hard copy. When it comes to our digital legacy, we would be wise to designate a digital executor who will spruce up our cyber selves for posterity and manage our digital estate. The digital executor should have access to our passwords and figure out how to close out or otherwise deal with our social media accounts and the contents of our computers, including our email. We will need to provide our digital executor with instructions about what we want permanently deleted, and for the data that remains, direction about who should have access and under what conditions. We'll need to get an agreement from our designate to take on this task, and make provision for the associated costs of this process.

Let's consider Facebook, for example. Some people turn the Facebook page of their deceased loved one into a digital memorial. Previous photos and posts stay visible, but no one can log in to the account. Depending on the privacy settings of the account, friends can share memories. Is this something you would want? If not, current Facebook policy allows you to choose a setting that will permanently delete your account in the event of your death. Websites like *DeadSocial* have resources to help you prepare for death on social media sites.[38] Given the pace of digital change and the impossibility of anticipating every issue, we may be wise to leave our digital executor with some general principles and trust her to use her best judgment.

Sir Terry Pratchett wanted to make sure his digital assets were destroyed, so he directed his executor to have his hard drive run over by a steamroller. Pratchett was an English author of fantasy novels who sold more than 85 million books, with a popularity at one point second only to that of J. K. Rowling, author of the blockbuster Harry Potter series. He died in 2015 at the age of sixty-six, after a long battle with Alzheimer's. After his diagnosis at the age of fifty-nine, Pratchett campaigned for dementia awareness and spearheaded the making of the documentary *Terry Pratchett: Choosing to Die*, which examines whether people could "arrange for themselves the death that they want."[39] His death was reported as natural and unassisted.[40]

Pratchett had considerable opportunity to think about both his legacy and his failing capacity, and when it came to the disposition of his digital files, he left nothing to chance. Pratchett directed in his will that "whatever he was working on at the time of his death [be] taken out along with his computers, to be put in the middle of a road and for a steamroller to steamroll over them all."[41] It is thought that ten incomplete novels were flattened and, although Pratchett himself didn't document his rationale, it was speculated that he didn't want his unpublished works to be completed by someone else and released. The man who oversaw the task is quoted as saying, "It's surprisingly difficult to find somebody to run over a hard drive with a steamroller." As it turned out, Pratchett's hard drive was tough enough to survive the steamroller attack and needed to be put in a stone crusher to finish the job.[42]

When we're considering whether to wipe our digital slate clean after our death, it's worthwhile considering the experience of Nick Bilton, who spent fourteen years writing about technology for the *New York Times*. When Bilton is looking for inspiration, he visits the Twitter page of his deceased colleague David Carr because his old tweets are "filled with nuggets of wisdom, humorous insights and deft turns of phrase." Bilton's deceased mother is still a "favourite" on his phone, he follows her on Facebook, and he saves her emails in his inbox, along with a video telling him how to make chocolate cake. What these technologies do, he says, is "connect us to people who are not with us, geographically or physically, and make us feel a little less alone in this big confusing world."[43] Maybe our digital legacy could keep us "alive" even after death, and like Bilton's digital contacts, we could still be providing inspiration and comfort to others from the afterlife.

While it's one thing for people to use our own words to maintain a connection with us after we're gone, it's quite another to put words into our mouths. This is happening with chatbots that are using artificial intelligence (AI) to help us live forever as their version of our digital selves. This idea may sound far-fetched, but we're using chatbots when we ask the computer-generated assistants Siri or Alexa to help us find out what movies are playing nearby or what the weather will be like tomorrow. So, there's a good chance AI will be used to keep some of us "alive." And, if we're going to be immortalized in a chatbot, we'd better leave detailed records of what we

really think. Otherwise, AI will fill the gap with its own con-
structs of our thoughts.

Data scientist Muhammad Aurangzeb Ahmad developed a
"griefbot" so his future children would have a chance to "meet"
their deceased grandfather. The computer-based chatbot uses
a text-based dialogue of questions and answers to permit his
descendants to "chat" with their grandfather. Before his father
died, Ahmad transcribed conversations between himself and his
father and used this dialogue as the basis for the simulation.
The bot uses AI to predict the grandfather's imagined responses
to new questions. Ahmad would like to expand the griefbot's
capabilities using voice synthesis and, eventually, virtual reality.
Ahmad acknowledges that we don't know who owns the rights
to create a simulation of a person, but that isn't stopping him.
"Why is it that we can't create simulations of people so they can
interact with others after they are gone?" he asks.[44]

You don't need to be a data scientist like Ahmad to create
some version of his griefbot. When James Vlahos's father was
diagnosed with a terminal illness, Vlahos began a conventional
oral history project by recording his dad telling stories and
singing songs. After Vlahos transcribed the recordings, rather
than compile a large binder of the written material, he decided
to create a "Dadbot" by feeding the material into a software
program. Vlahos does not have a computer coding background
and says the program lets someone like him craft an interac-
tive conversational character. He says he isn't under any delu-
sion that he's created "a robot version of my dad from science

fiction." "Like, my real dad is gone," he says, "and I and the family have to mourn that. But I have created something that shares nice memories of him and brings him to life, I hope, in little vivid ways."[45] James Vlahos wrote an article for *Wired* magazine that documents his journey producing the Dadbot.[46]

The potential for a more full-bodied digital legacy of ourselves was foreshadowed by the concert appearance in 2012 of groundbreaking American rapper and actor Tupac Shakur. What was disconcerting about Shakur's performance at the Coachella music festival in Indio, California, was the fact that he had died in a shooting fifteen years earlier at age twenty-five. A "hologram" of the deceased Shakur shared the stage with fellow rappers Dr. Dre and Snoop Dogg to perform two of Shakur's bestselling songs. The "hologram" was more accurately a 2D projection pulled together by using old footage of Tupac's performances to create an animation that incorporated characteristics of his movements.[47] According to people who were present, the simulation was incredibly lifelike, and media reported that Tupac's mother, who had given her permission for the resurrection, was "positively thrilled" with the virtual performance.[48] Asher Underwood, founder of the forum Truth about Tupac, said reaction from other people was mixed. "Where some feel it's exploitive of Pac, many others—especially the fans—are just happy to see Pac's legacy still being kept alive." The hologram was given its own Twitter account and there was talk of taking it on a world tour.[49] In 2017, Tupac was inducted into the US Rock and Roll Hall of Fame as a more one-dimensional record of his legacy. Snoop Dogg accepted the honour on his behalf, saying, "You will live on forever."[50]

Stephen Hawking, the brilliant physicist who died in 2018, realized his afterlife could take on a digital life of its own and tried to exert some control over his own persona. Many people would immediately recognize Hawking's distinctive computer-generated voice from his guest appearances on TV shows like *The Simpsons* and *The Big Bang Theory*, if not from his lectures on his bestselling book *A Brief History of Time*. Hawking lived much of his life with a motor neuron disease and lost his voice in 1985 after a tracheotomy. When the technology for his computerized voice box needed an update in 2011, Hawking was determined to maintain his original digitized sound. Lama Nachman headed up the team that did the upgrade, and she told CBC Radio that although newer computerized voices had become available, Hawking insisted on keeping the one he had. He felt strongly the software voice he had gained in 1986 was his own and had it copyrighted so that he (or his estate) could control who was putting words into his mouth.[51]

I've talked about recording our narrative ourselves to try and control our afterlife, but ultimately, that control is limited. Our legacy will assume a life of its own. After our death, our image may be improved or we could experience a fall from grace. Bad acts may catch up with us, or good behaviour that went unrecognized may find the light of day. History will have its way with us—for better or worse—as we'll see in the next chapter.

History Will Have Its Way with Us

Despite our best efforts to control our afterlife, history will draw its own conclusions about our legacy. Our reputation may rise or fall with the judgments of future times. On the upside, behaviour that is viewed as scandalous in one era may become acceptable, if not the norm. We've watched that happen during our lifetime with issues such as out-of-wedlock pregnancy, sexual orientation and assisted dying. On the downside, secrets can emerge from dusty closets to discolour people's images in the eyes of their descendants or society at large. There might be revelations of ill-gotten gains, neglected responsibilities, cruelty, sexism, racism or crime. The following stories remind us that our best recourse is to live what we understand to be a good life. But we'd be wise to look in the mirror of judgment from time to time, preferably the magnifying side with its unforgiving reflection.

Our Pasts Catch Up with Us

As society evolves, deeper application of standards of human rights and common decency can result in revised judgments in the courts of public and private opinion. Over the decades, the chipping of names off buildings, toppling of statues and removal of plaques have provided us with vivid images of history's verdict. Universities are often a battleground for reputational revisions, because students are demanding that our institutions of learning walk their talk and live their values. In 2017, the University of Victoria removed the name of Joseph Trutch from a residence building because "his attitude to indigenous peoples was particularly negative even for his time." Trutch was a nineteenth-century commissioner of lands and works and BC's first lieutenant-governor. In announcing the decision, the university said that Trutch's actions regarding the land rights of First Nations and his disregard for their concerns conflicted with the university's mission, vision and values.[1] Historians were well aware of Trutch's legacy, having included him in their 2007 "Top Ten Worst Canadians," a list compiled by the history magazine the *Beaver*.[2]

Yale University made a similar decision in 2017 in renaming one of its undergraduate colleges. Calhoun College was named in 1933 to honour the legacy of John C. Calhoun, a former US vice president and senator from South Carolina before the Civil War. He was also a slave owner. In announcing the decision, Yale's president said, "John C. Calhoun's legacy as a white supremacist and a national leader who passionately promoted slavery as a 'positive good' fundamentally conflicts with Yale's mission and values." As Calhoun's past caught up with his afterlife, history refocused the spotlight on a deserving role model. Calhoun College has been renamed Grace Hopper College in recognition of Grace Murray Hopper, a pioneering computer scientist who graduated from Yale in the 1930s.[3]

Some bad actors are still alive to watch as their legacies are rewritten. In 2005, Queen's University stripped David Radler's name from a wing of its business school. Radler was sixty-three years old and had just pleaded guilty in a US District Court to charges connected with a $32-million fraud at Hollinger International Inc., part of a criminal probe that included Conrad Black and other former executives. Radler had received the naming recognition in 2000 after pledging a million dollars to Queen's. The university concluded that the integrity of the gift had been compromised and returned the money. Radler had a long history with Queen's; both he and his father were graduates. It's believed to be the first time a Canadian charitable organization returned a gift because a donor later committed a crime.[4]

But if our bad behaviour can catch up with us, so can the good. We have the earlier example of Grace Hopper, whose scientific legacy was finally acknowledged by Yale University. On International Women's Day, March 8, 2018, the *New York Times* launched a project to celebrate other overlooked heroines. Since 1851, the vast majority of obituaries published by the newspaper documented the lives of white men. To redress the balance, "Overlooked" will be a regular feature of the obituary section that will shine a light on the women over the centuries who left indelible marks and deserve to have a testament to their contributions. The program began with fifteen obituaries, including ones for Sylvia Plath (whose story you read earlier); Ida B. Wells, an investigative reporter who campaigned against lynching; and Qiu Jin, a feminist poet and revolutionary who became an advocate for women's liberation in China. Readers are being encouraged to nominate candidates who should be included. Amisha Padnani is the journalist who developed this concept as a way to give remarkable women their due. She wrote, "I'm hopeful it will inspire many more conversations inside the newsroom and beyond about diversity and what we can do to make sure no one is overlooked."[5]

James Baldwin

A stellar example of revitalizing and solidifying a legacy is the project undertaken by Raoul Peck to immortalize the powerful words of writer and social critic James Baldwin. Peck is a Haitian filmmaker and political activist who was introduced to Baldwin's writings as a teenager, and his words burned their messages into his brain. Peck is certainly not the only keeper of Baldwin's flame, but his 2017 documentary, *I Am Not Your Negro*, lit a bonfire under Baldwin's legacy.

Baldwin died in 1987 at the age of sixty-three, and thirty years later, Peck brought him back to life by letting him tell his own story. Every word spoken in the two-hour film is Baldwin's, either through archival footage or voice-over narration of his writing. As well, Peck introduces us to new material held by Baldwin's estate, thirty pages of *Remember This House*, a manuscript that Baldwin was working on before his death. The unfinished book was to be his reflections on three assassinated civil rights leaders: Malcolm X, Martin Luther King Jr. and Medgar Evers.

The film was ten years in the making. In a 2017 CBC Radio interview, Peck described making the film as a "very heavy burden." "I had to make the film that would establish Baldwin as the important man, thinker, philosopher, witness, political analyst, et cetera, that he is," he said, "because people were starting to forget about him—to forget about his role in the history of civil rights, his examination of racism in America, the way he deconstructs the image of the American dream. Nobody will ever again forget who James Baldwin was, and that was my agenda."[6] In his review in the *New York Review of Books*, the writer Darryl Pinckney describes the film as "a kind of tone poem to a freedom movement not yet finished." "Peck's commitment to Baldwin's voice is total," he wrote.[7]

While Baldwin had Peck working singlehandedly to reignite his legacy, the British nineteenth-century author Jane Austen had hundreds of thousands of fans who turned her candles of memory into a forest fire of immortalization.

Jane Austen

Jane Austen died two centuries ago and her legacy has been raging apace ever since. She wrote six major novels, including *Pride and Prejudice* and *Sense and Sensibility*, and even if you haven't read her books, you may have seen the film and television adaptations. You can buy Jane Austen paraphernalia, from tea-cups to sweatshirts, or read academic essays, biographies or even a "sequel." If you want to go all out, you can don a Regency costume and attend a Janeite convention, tea party or ball. And, if you get your hands on a 2013 issue of a British ten-pound note, you'll likely find Austen's face.

Given all this exposure, you might be surprised to learn that when Austen died in 1817 at age forty-one, her family went to serious efforts to control and sanitize her image. They put themselves in charge of her legacy with the goal of creating an official portrait of piety and restraint that was appropriate for an unmarried woman of the time. The majority of Austen's letters were destroyed or censored, most at the hands of her sister. Initially, two family-authored books set the tone for Austen's reputation: a memoir written by her nephew and a collection of letters published by her great-nephew. Austen was "Aunt Jane" to these men, and Devoney Looser explains in *The Making of Jane Austen* how their works "promoted their author-ancestor as a very particular kind of aunt—the cheerful, pious, domestic, polite, maiden aunt." Austen's nephew describes his aunt's life as "singularly barren . . . of events."[8]

While the Austen family portrayed their Jane as a conservative gentlewoman who led a quiet, sheltered life, Paula Byrne points out in *The Real Jane Austen* that the truth veered sharply from this picture. Far from being a country mouse, Austen spent much of her life in the city. She was actually well travelled and even used the public transport of the day—the stagecoach.

According to the nephew-authored memoir, Austen's clerical brother formed and directed her taste in reading, but according to Byrne, she required no such teacher. Moreover, Byrne says the nephew's memoir is humourless, further supporting the family-constructed portrait of a dour spinster. As Byrne says, "Jane Austen was one of the wittiest of writers, but there are not many jokes in the official family record."[9]

Over time, Austen's legacy would fly free from the family grasp, and people would use their own interpretations and agendas to remake Austen in their own likeness. In the process, she became a woman for all seasons, either a champion of domestic values resisting social change or a feminist reimagining women's role. As Looser says, "Each group saw its image of Austen as the right one, although these versions of the author couldn't have been more different . . . In some situations, and at some moments, Austen has been presented as gloriously conservative. At others, she's described as unflinchingly progressive."[10]

The imagining and reimagining of Austen's legacy continues apace. Writing in the *New Yorker* in 2017, Anthony Lane urges us to read Austen's final novel, *Sanditon*, both to understand more about Austen's never-discussed love life and because the novel is an "exercise in courage." Austen wrote the manuscript when her health was failing, and Lane says it is precisely because she was dying that the book "brims with life." "The result is robust, unsparing, and alert to all the latest fashions in human foolishness," Lane says.[11] The title of Lane's review is

"Last Laugh," a descriptor that sums up Austen's relationship to her legacy. When we talk about the real Jane Austen, we'll never know if we got it right, but all these years later, we're still talking about her.

In the next chapter, we'll examine how we shape our legacy through instructions to be executed after our death and why it's important that our directions be carefully thought out. When wills are left undone or estates badly handled, the most beloved memory can be besmirched. Even if we have lived stellar lives, we can tarnish our legacies by leaving our affairs in a mess and forcing others to struggle to clean things up after we're gone. Living a good life isn't enough; we need to pay attention to our afterlife.

Instructions from the Grave

The stories you're about to read have convinced me that I need to have a will, I need to pay careful attention to what my will says, and I need to discuss the contents of my will with my loved ones. I know this is all easier said than done. We have understandable reasons for avoiding writing a will. In some cases, we think we have no estate—nothing of value that needs distributing to others. In other cases, writing a will requires us to make difficult decisions about the distribution of our estate, and we're waiting for the issues to magically resolve themselves. In some cases, we think we have a will but we haven't taken the steps necessary to turn a written statement of our wishes into a legal will. Some of us are ducking the duty of will-writing in the hopes "it will all work out." This is often short form for admitting that any fallout from our negligence won't matter to us—after all, we'll be dead.

One persuasive reason for paying attention to the affairs of our afterlife is to protect the legacy we develop when we are alive. We know that our positive image can be jeopardized by the mess we leave behind because of something called "the peak-end rule." The rule was developed by psychologist Daniel Kahneman to explain foibles in our memory. According to Kahneman's research, the way an experience ends determines our memories of the event and the level of associated happiness.[1] When we apply this rule to our legacy, if our family and friends struggle to find our bank accounts, are hurt by unequal treatment in our will, or are left to fight with one another over our possessions, the goodwill we generated over a lifetime could be overwritten by feelings of resentment and frustration. Conversely, as Shakespeare understood, "all's well that ends well." So the warm glow we generate by treating with consideration and kindness those who have to deal with our affairs could replace people's negative assessment of our lives, or at least soften the sting.

The stories in this chapter are cautionary tales that help us think through what we're trying to do with our will. They raise issues we may otherwise overlook, and highlight the complexities of some decisions. These shared experiences put us in a better position to instruct our lawyer or to draft our own wills to get the results we want for ourselves. But these stories are no substitute for legal advice. And when you're reading about others' experiences, remember that wills and estates are not governed by Canada's national laws. They are under provincial and territorial jurisdiction, and you need to inform yourself about the specific legislation that applies to you.

Do I Need a Will?

If we die without a will (the legal term is intestate), we forfeit the right to choose what happens to our possessions. Along with losing control of who benefits from our estate, we may subject any beneficiaries to a lengthy and expensive legal process. Our estate will be divided according to provincial legislation and allocations will be made to next of kin according to a family tree including spouse, children and moving on to other relatives. Generally speaking, if you die without a spouse or children, your estate goes to your parents, and if your parents are deceased, it goes to your siblings. If a sibling is dead, their share goes to their children and so on down to increasingly remote relatives you don't even know. You may find this a boring listing of legalese until you substitute these labels with your own relatives and think about them inheriting your hard-earned money rather than people of your own choosing.

Lawyers Jean Blacklock and Sarah Kruger have written a Canadian guide to estate-planning mistakes. They warn that if you allow your estate to be distributed according to this "cookie-cutter formula," "all hell can break loose." Here are some of their examples: People you don't like may inherit some of your assets, such as a spouse from whom you've been separated for many years and never divorced. Laws in most provinces don't fully recognize common-law spouses, so when it comes to dying without a will, your relationship may not be on the same footing as a legal marriage. Your underage children could become entitled to money that a public trustee or guardian will manage until they reach the age of majority. At that point, Blacklock and Kruger warn, "Some teenagers we know (cough, cough) would invest the funds in a new Hummer the day they got the cheque."[2]

When I interviewed Gloria, she told me a painful story that illustrates what can happen if we die intestate. "My friend had two young children, and when we were chatting one day, she told me she didn't have a will," Gloria recalls. "I urged her to do something about it. I was particularly concerned because I knew she had an abusive spouse. My friend confessed she couldn't bear to think about death for fear of bringing it on. As it turned out, her lack of a will created a disaster. My friend died suddenly and her husband took all her money and left the children destitute. She believed that nothing bad could happen if she didn't think about it, and boy, was she wrong."

At thirty-four, Meredith has two young children and tells her friends to put writing a will on their to-do list. "To act otherwise is very irresponsible," she says. "I'm always amazed at the number of people who don't think about what will happen after they die and don't care. How can you not care? If you don't have a will, settling your estate could take forever. It could go to the courts and you don't know what the outcome will be. By doing your will, you make everyone's life easier."

Meredith says that having children brought this issue to the forefront for her, but it was a struggle to bring her husband on board. "My husband said, 'I don't need a will. Why would it matter, I'm going to be dead.' So, I had to go to the lawyer's office by myself. When I got there, I decided to have a draft of a will prepared for my husband as well as the one for me. When I brought the document home, he said, 'That's not how I want it.' So, he changed it the way he wanted, and this is how I finally got him to write his will."

"Writing a will isn't enough," she warns. "You have to sign it and have it properly witnessed and turn it into a legal document. I can't believe the number of people I know who say 'I have a will. My lawyer drew it up and I haven't signed it yet.' This is not a legal will. When it comes to making your will, done is better than perfect. It is better to have some control than absolutely none. You can always go back and change it. The only downside is you pay some legal fees. Hiring a good lawyer or notary public is worth the effort because it makes you think about the complications. If you're not working with a good lawyer, you're going to forget something."

Is My Will Legally Binding?

Meredith could have been addressing her remarks to John. Four or five years ago, John instructed his lawyer to draft his will, and it now sits in his drawer, unsigned. "The way the will is written just doesn't feel right," he says. John is in his late sixties and has been with the same partner for twenty years. They live together but are not married and have maintained separate financial lives with the intent of preserving a type of independence. John's story illustrates the tough decisions that underlie drawing up a will and why procrastination can seem so attractive. "I have known for a long time that this deserves my attention, but knowing this hasn't made me move on it," he says.

John describes his dilemma: "I have lived in my house for forty years, and half of that time my partner has been living with me, so it has become his home. He's fourteen years younger than me, so I assume I'll predecease him, which informs my thinking on the will. My partner is estranged from his family and he has become part of my extended family. He's working and has a good pension. His financial security is in sharp contrast to that of my impoverished sister and her son, who've been bumping along the bottom. Our mother didn't leave a big estate and there won't be enough money to bail out my sister." In addition to these financial considerations, John has some charitable causes he'd like to support as part of his legacy.

"At this point, I can't figure things out. I'm looking for strategies," he says. When I ask John if he has talked to his partner about his conflicted thinking, he replies, "Yes, but not enough." John concludes our conversation by saying he is going to sit down with his partner and come to an understanding that he will use as a basis for a redrafted will. "I know I need to have a legally binding will," he says.

From time to time, we hear about a case that reminds us to make certain our will is written and witnessed in a manner that makes it legally binding. One such case was decided in 2017 in the province of British Columbia after going all the way to the BC Court of Appeal. The case involved the $1.3-million estate of a ninety-three-year-old widow named Eleanor Hadley. A few months before she died, she had handwritten what she titled "my last Will" in her journal, naming two friends as beneficiaries along with a niece. She had an earlier official will that allocated her estate differently. The courts concluded that "my last Will" did not represent Hadley's final wishes because she did not tell anyone about it, the document had not been witnessed, and she did not repudiate her earlier will.

An unsuccessful appeal to recognize "my last Will" was launched by Daniel Pierce, a filmmaker and beneficiary of this version of Hadley's will. The court ruled in favour of the official will and decided that everyone's legal expenses should be paid by Hadley's estate, since it was her conduct that had triggered the litigation.[3] We can't be sure of Hadley's wishes, but she certainly would have been disturbed by the amount of her estate that was eaten up in legal fees. The case generated a great deal of media attention, including a CBC Radio phone-in show. A caller to the show said people should have a will; otherwise, they will leave astronomical family conflicts. In the caller's family, two siblings no longer speak to one another because their mother died without a will.[4]

Where Are My Documents?

As Hadley's story illustrates, it's not enough to have a legal will; people need to know that we have a will and where it's located. As well, we need to leave the details of our complete financial picture where someone can find them. I was the executor of my father's estate, and when he died, I was extremely grateful he had his affairs in good order. He developed dementia in his later years and hadn't updated his information, so there were a few wrinkles. His list of bank accounts included some that he'd already closed, for example. And I had to authorize the bank to break into his safety deposit box because I couldn't find the key. But while he was in sound mind, Dad had been extremely thorough. By the way, the Bank of Canada reports that as of 2016, they are holding 1.8 million unclaimed bank balances, worth some $678 million. If you think yours might be among them, they have a searchable registry of unclaimed balances.[5]

I had a good overview of Dad's assets because I had been doing his taxes in his later years; otherwise, I would have wanted to see copies of his tax returns. I knew about his pension and retirement plans and insurance policies. By the time Dad died, he'd sold his house and car; otherwise, I would have needed proof of ownership. I had his birth certificate, marriage licence and other official documents, as well as his user names and passwords. I had the paper proof and certificates for his stocks and bonds. The biggest bonus was that I had already formed a good working relationship with Dad's financial adviser. Here's where I can attest to the power of the peak-end rule described earlier. I'd always loved my father deeply. But because of his consideration around his estate, his star burned even more brightly for me as I struggled to work through these details in the midst of my grief.

In contrast, Dorothy's husband was firmly in death denial. When he dropped dead of a heart attack at age sixty-six, he left her with a financial mess that took months and months of dedicated effort to clean up. "My husband had survived some near brushes with death, and you'd think that might have made him more conscious of his mortality," Dorothy says, "but that's not how it worked. Instead, he thought of himself as a survivor. He was always a person who pushed the limits. So, when he died, nothing was written down. He had fourteen bank accounts and I didn't have signing authority for any of them. He had set up several companies and I didn't know what they were. He had an insurance policy that he had let lapse a few months before his death. He didn't think he was near the end. Even to begin dealing with his estate, I needed our marriage certificate, and I couldn't find it. So, I had to apply for a marriage certificate as a widow. It was a nightmare. I learned a painful lesson. So now, when I 'go,' I'm going to leave everything in place."

Does Asking Mean Getting?

When we're writing our wills, here's an important reminder: just because we request something doesn't always mean it will happen. Sometimes our wishes are unreasonable, impractical or likely to cause hardship, or are unenforceable. Sometimes, for example, we are making our request of an organization with no legal requirement to honour our wishes. This was the case for the British-born conservationist Archibald Belaney, better known by his fraudulent First Nations identity Grey Owl. Belaney and his wife took on responsibility for two orphaned beaver kits, which they named Jelly Roll and Rawhide.

In 1931, while working as a caretaker of park animals at Prince Albert National Park in Saskatchewan, he built a small log cabin beside Ajawaan Lake for the two beavers and their four kits. He named the cabin "Beaver Lodge," and it became a great tourist attraction for summer visitors to the park. The author Frances Backhouse visited the lodge while researching her book *Once They Were Hats: In Search of the Mighty Beaver* and watched some old film footage of Belaney playing with his beavers. Backhouse writes about Belaney's "unreserved affection" for the animals, "the tenderness with which he bottle-feeds tiny, fuzzy kits; his frank pleasure when he wrestles with one of the adults."[6]

In 1938, Belaney died of pneumonia at age forty-nine. Backhouse wondered what had happened to Jelly Roll and Rawhide when they lost their benefactor. She learned that Belaney, in his will, had asked his employers to care for Jelly Roll and Rawhide until they died. This was not an inexpensive undertaking, and it was especially challenging during the Depression, when budgets were tight. Backhouse reports, "It wasn't unusual for Grey Owl's monthly grocery order to include 50 pounds of rice, 40 loaves of whole-wheat bread, 10 pounds of peanuts, five crates of apples and a box of chocolate bars—with most of these provisions destined for the beavers."[7]

Instead of honouring Belaney's last request, the National Parks Bureau controller decided to quietly cut off the beavers' support system and leave them to fend for themselves. When fans of the beavers wrote to ask about the animals' welfare, they were told they had "reverted to their wild state, but can still be seen by parties visiting the lake." Backhouse calls out this falsehood. By this time, she writes, Rawhide had not been seen for years and Jelly Roll's fate was equally unknown.[8] During her visit to Beaver Lodge in 2011, Backhouse didn't see any beavers.

The case of Jelly Roll and Rawhide has something to teach us about the fate of our pets if we depart this earth abruptly. Leaving directions for our pet's welfare in our will is an important step in being a responsible owner. But first, we need to get the consent of our designated caregivers and determine that they are up to the task.

What about My Remains?

Some of us use our will to make requests regarding disposal of our remains, and some of those wishes can prove challenging to honour. When the architectural historian Christopher Gray died in 2017 at the age of sixty-six, his lawyer informed his family that he had bequeathed his skeleton to his high school alma mater in Concord, New Hampshire, for display in the science lab. Gray had been thorough in his preparation and had even tracked down a company that provided skull-cleaning services, mainly for hunters preserving their game. But when Gray's family approached the company after Gray's death, it refused to do the job for Gray's skeleton. The family was determined to honour Gray's wish and came up with a complicated plan that involved donating his remains to the Smithsonian, which agreed to clean up the skeleton and then loan it to the high school on a long-term basis. The school's biology teacher is thrilled with the gift. "I'm hoping I can learn more about this alum," she says. "I want to hear his story so I can share it with the students. It really makes the science come alive."[9]

When I interviewed Stewart about the legacy of his best friend, Dave, he talked about being given the responsibility for distributing Dave's ashes. Stewart and Dave had been friends since fourth grade. They marched ceremonial flags together as Boy Scouts, and while they were in the navy, their ships sailed side by side. "Dave died of a brain tumour when he was sixty-nine," Stewart says. "I never thought I'd be washing my best friend's body as he lay dying. He was dead within a year of diagnosis. Dave taught fourth and fifth grades, and then became a principal. He had five children. His legacy is his children, his grandchildren and the thousands of children he educated to love learning. His relationship with his students was more like a great father than a teacher. He was a phenomenal human being. All his life, he was doing supportive things. He knew he'd done his work and died with that knowledge."

After Dave's funeral, family and friends gathered for a reception at the home of one of Dave's children. Stewart acted as moderator as people told their stories about Dave. It was at the reception that one of Dave's children told Stewart about Dave's last request. Dave had directed in his will that Stewart should distribute his ashes "in beautiful places." "This was the first I heard of this," Stewart says. "I had watched as Dave's ashes were placed in the cemetery site where his mother's ashes were buried. But, it turned out that was only some of his ashes. The balance was placed in a beautiful handcrafted wooden container that Dave had made himself. And that container was to be turned over to me."

Dave had chosen well when he selected Stewart for this responsibility. "I don't see this as a burden," Stewart says. "I feel it is an honour. Dave has been dead for three years now, and over that time, I've left ashes in maybe a dozen spots. Each time, I've had a little ceremony. I say a prayer and light a candle. I don't plan the locations in advance—it just hits me in certain places. Sometimes, I discover the perfect spot and then go back to get the ashes. I left some on a remote island in the dead of winter; some I scattered on a mountaintop; some I placed in an old-growth cedar tree in a cathedral grove; and some I spread on a beautiful beach in Hawaii. I'm videotaping the process. After I've distributed all the ashes and compiled the footage from all the sites, I'll make a video and send it to Dave's children." When it comes to his own death, Stewart says he's got a plan: "I'm giving my body to science."

Some people feel that, since they own nothing of value, they don't need a will. The next sections remind us that value is subjective and an item can hold an emotional importance that bears no proportion to its monetary value. Families can fight over trinkets; if you address the allocation of these mementos, either before your death or as part of your will, you might help keep the peace.

What about My Stuff?

A will explains how we want our stuff distributed. People get sidetracked by the heft of the word *estate*, and we'd probably have more people writing wills if we substituted it with the word *stuff*. Virtually all of us leave something when we die—if it's not property or money, it may be personal belongings. And our personal belongings may have deep meaning to someone. Sometimes, people include a list in the will itself that allocates major items. Some people compile an itemized list as a separate document and refer to the list's existence in the will. A separate document has the benefit of being easy to update over time.

Allocating your stuff may seem onerous, but if you don't handle this task with care, you can leave lifelong rifts of resentment. A lawyer told me how frustrating it was to watch a family feud that eventually went to litigation over a sixty-five-dollar cornflower glass plate. "These things can have deep sentimental attachments," she says. "People equate what you left them with how much you love them."

Carole saw this problem first-hand when her parents died, and she is working hard not to repeat the problems of the past. "Designating things in advance is the right thing to do," she says. "Now, years later, there is still a lot of resentment in my family because my sister swooped in and took all the best china out of my mother's house right after her death. Also, my parents told me they wanted me to have the dining-room table that we sat around for years, but it's with my niece. We get emotionally invested in certain things. So, I'm doing things differently. I'm going to ask our children what they want and I'll make a list."

Carole says her goal during the allocation process is to be clear, responsible and communicative. "I want their memories of me and their father to remain positive," she says, "and this will all depend on the way we handle this issue. It's tempting to just say, 'They'll sort it out' or 'They can wrestle over that vase.' I don't think they'll do that very easily. Once I've got this nailed down, I'll feel a lot better. After all, my husband and I could walk out of here and get hit by a bus. Obviously, I'm not counting on that happening, but I'd like things to be in place, just in case."

George told me the story of how his grandmother distributed her possessions, describing what the process looked like from the receiving end. He remembers the distribution taking place at a family gathering at his grandmother's home. George is now thirty years old; he was a young boy at the time. "My grandfather had died some time before," he recalls, "and I was with my mother, my older sister, and my aunt and uncle (my mother's siblings). My grandmother gave everyone a stack of Post-it notes and asked us to go around the house and put our name on anything we wanted. Names were put into a hat to decide the order that people would make their choices."

George remembers being uncomfortable at the time. He chose some small items to remind him of his grandfather— little toys and memorabilia. "These things were from the 'rumpus room' in the basement," he says. "This was my retreat, my special place to play and hang out." After his grandmother died a few years ago, he received the things he had requested. One item was a large glass jar with hundreds of swizzle sticks of every imaginable shape and colour, which his grandparents had collected from their trips. "It sounds pretty kitschy," he says, "but it's actually very cool."

Recently, George's aunt told him that her husband was very interested in the swizzle stick collection, as well as some other items George had received. She wondered whether he would be interested in giving them up. But George wants to hang on to them. "In truth, they don't mean much to me now," he says, "but they did at one time and they may again. In general, I don't like hanging on to stuff, but I'm making an exception with these things."

Even though the distribution was done a few years ago, George's mother still talks about how, when it came time to divvy things up, some items were missing. She blamed his aunt. "But all in all, it worked more or less," George says. "The older I get, the more impressed I am that my grandmother bit the bullet. She had the gumption to push the issue and try and resolve this distribution of her stuff in a fair and reasonable manner. She made her best effort to minimize the battles after she was gone."

What If I Don't Allocate My Things?

Joshua Harmon's brilliant play *Bad Jews* illustrates eloquently how an item can become a stand-in for love and respect, and how a tug of war over its ownership can exacerbate family fissures.[10] The setting is a New York apartment after the funeral of a beloved grandfather. As his three grandchildren gather, we learn that one of Poppy's possessions is imbued with intense meaning for them: his chai. *Chai* is the Hebrew word for "life," and Poppy wore his gold pendant chai on a chain around his neck. The chai had belonged to Poppy's father, and during the Holocaust, when his father knew they would be separated, he gave his son the chai. Poppy managed to survive the concentration camp and was able to keep his chai hidden under his tongue for the two years of his internment.

Granddaughter Daphna, who self-defines as "the most religious" of the group, states that it is the only thing of her grandfather's she wants. She argues that the chai should be hers because she's the only one who would value it. She acknowledges that a chai is typically worn by men but points out that it is technically a piece of jewellery. But it turns out that her cousin Liam already has the chai in his possession. Liam says his mother gave him the chai because "everyone knew" that Poppy wanted him to have it, and besides, Poppy's things are men's things and should go to men. Liam, who calls himself a "bad Jew," dismisses Daphna's argument that the chai should go to her because it is a religious item. He says the chai is "so much more" and mattered to Poppy on "a whole host of different levels." Liam says Poppy would have wanted him to have the chai so he could use it to propose to his girlfriend in the same way Poppy used the chai to propose to their grandmother.

Liam's girlfriend, Melody, is a Gentile, and the battle over the chai becomes a deep debate about culture and identity and survival, until it deteriorates into a physical altercation with Daphna ripping the chai off Melody's neck. Even before the chai tug-of-war, the cousins didn't like each other much. But as the play ends, their ruptured relationships seem beyond repair. Poppy never bequeathed the chai in his will and what is missing in this debate is any direct evidence of his wishes. In Daphna's words, ". . . when my mom talked to your mom she was like the kids should work it out, because apparently as it turns out Poppy's will is like basically useless which I don't blame him for, at all, but like, no one actually realized that someone would have to actually figure this stuff out at some point but it's like that point is now here."[11]

Regardless of the arguments in favour of allocating your possessions in order to avoid a family fracas, some people would rather leave items up for grabs. Sometimes the incentive is to avoid any hint of favouritism. To Alison's surprise, this has turned out to be her daughter's strategy regarding Alison's three grandchildren. Of the three, one is Alison's namesake. Alison has a collection of silver spoons, engraved with either her name or her initials, which she had been given as a child. "I mentioned to my daughter, in passing," she says, "that I was going to designate in my will that these keepsakes go to the granddaughter who shares my name. My thinking was sentimental but also practical. I couldn't imagine anyone but this granddaughter using silverware with these initials. My daughter was adamant that I must not single out the one grandchild. Although I think my approach was both appropriate and logical, I'll drop the idea. To avoid my daughter's ire, I'll honour her wishes and let them work it out after I'm gone."

What about a Family Cottage?

We can't talk about dispersing our meaningful things without talking about the family cottage. When people share horror stories about a legacy of family breakdowns, battles over a cottage take centre stage. The getaway may have been in the family for generations or newly purchased, it may be a shack or a mansion, it may be actively used or abandoned, but chances are good that the cottage is imbued with intense feelings. Claire's story sets out the classic dilemma.

"I'm eighty-eight years old and my husband is ninety, and when it comes to legacy," Claire says, "the big problem is the cottage. It's on my mind all the time. We have owned the cottage for fifty-five years, through four generations, and I've been up there every summer all summer for many years. I have three children and six grandchildren, and I would like nothing better than to keep the cottage going for them forever. But it makes no sense. The cottage costs twenty-thousand dollars per year to maintain, and the two children who could afford to maintain it are the least likely to use it. When the grandchildren were young, they used to be there all summer, but now, they're at camp or they're working. This summer, we will be alone except for some weekends, and the kids are hysterical with worry about us being there on our own."

Claire says that the cottage is continuously on her mind and causes her enormous anxiety. "I can't talk about it with the family," she says, "because it upsets everyone. All these years, my friends have been giving up their cottages, and now I understand the turmoil. So, I've decided to bite the bullet. I'm going to sell the cottage. It's chockablock filled with our art, furniture and my mother's silver, and I'm selling it 'as is' except for the silver. This may break my heart but it's time."

The stories are legion about cases where a cottage is left in the will as a legacy to be shared among family members. In exceptional cases, this seems to work out. But many families have been defeated by the challenges of joint usage of a property, which include collecting money from everyone for taxes, upkeep and repair; juggling schedules for usage by each family member; and reconciling conflicting standards of cleanliness and maintenance.

Deciding how to dispose of the cottage can raise its own set of problems. When my friend and her siblings were settling their deceased mother's estate, they had a fundamental disagreement over how the family's island retreat should be handled. My friend and her brother wanted the island to be donated to a land trust and preserved as a wilderness, and the other two siblings wanted the property to be sold for an astronomical sum to an eager property developer. Their lawyers negotiated a settlement, and the island ended up being divided permanently with half being developed and the other half set up as a nature reserve. The family divide was also permanent.

Carole describes yet another variation on the theme of cottages ripping families apart. "My grandparents owned a fine stretch of beach land with two cottages side by side," she says. "My mother used one cottage and her sister used the other." Carole remembers that her grandparents kept expanding and improving her mother's cottage, and that's where everyone stayed. In contrast, her aunt, who lived a good distance away, rarely used her cottage, and it was never improved. "I don't know what my grandmother's will said," Carole recalls, "but after she died, my aunt insisted that half of the big cottage was hers, in addition to her small cottage. And she did get both. She was a taker. I remember that immediately after Grandma died, my aunt cleared out all her antiques and a very valuable crystal vase. She carted it all away, insisting these things were hers. This whole thing ruptured the sisters' relationship forever." The situation Carole is describing happened decades ago, but her resentment is as raw as if it had taken place yesterday.

Estate planner Sandy Cardy wrote *The Cottage, the Spider Brooch, and the Second Wife* to give us some insight into how we might handle estate planning with more self-awareness and insight—and, hopefully, with some grace and compassion. Her book, written with Michael Fitzgerald, is a fictionalized account of the Hilroy family. As the story begins, Alfred Hilroy is a sixty-eight-year-old recent widower who has started dating a woman around the same age as his three children. The relationship raises red flags for the children, who are worried about their father's well-being, their mother's memory and their own happiness. Things progress rapidly and Alfred and his new love start making wedding plans. Due to a boating accident, Alfred's soon-to-be-wife does not want to spend time at the family cottage, and Alfred wants more money to travel and enjoy life with his beloved. So, without consulting his children, he initiates plans to sell the cottage. The result is the predictable family rupture with misunderstandings and resentments on all sides. Alfred recognizes he is in danger of losing his loving relationship with his children. Working with his lawyer, he comes up with a strategy for keeping the cottage but reducing its costs, as well as handling other items of contention, including the treasured spider brooch of the book title. Alfred's compromise reflects the children's concerns and is one that everyone can live with.

The happy ending for the Hilroy story may be fictional but the message is real-life. Alfred learns that he has to change his belief that estate and money matters should be kept private. He realizes he has to share his thinking and listen to others if he wants to keep his family intact. The book's biggest lesson is that cottages, and other significant family items, have a meaning for people that goes far deeper than monetary value, and you ignore these feelings at your peril.

As you'll read in the next section, unequal treatment of siblings is another matter that falls into the category of dangerous territory. These issues can have a significant impact on our legacy and we need to face them.

Does Unequal Treatment Matter?

The common advice is to handle gifts to your children as you wish while you're alive but to treat them equally in the will. The reasoning is that our children tend to measure the depth of our love by the amount of money or things we bequeath to them in the will. When Phyllis's father decided to divide his estate unevenly, he left a family rupture that has yet to heal. "I was the eldest, and I had two younger brothers," Phyllis says. "My father's estate was split two-fifths, two-fifths, one-fifth— with me getting the small share." Phyllis has no idea why her father made this decision, and she only found out about it when she read the will. She had never had a falling out with her father and thought he loved all his children equally. There wasn't a big difference in the siblings' financial circumstances that might account for the differential treatment.

Phyllis was so hurt by her father's action, she began to question her paternity. "My legacy was being treated differently and without explanation. It made me wonder if I was his daughter. I was a wartime baby and I actually considered trying to get my father's service record to find out if he was home at the right time to be my father."

Her father's decision also destroyed Phyllis's relationship with her brother. "My brother was the executor of my father's will," Phyllis says, "but his wife took on the responsibility. My brother is under the thumb of his wife, who handles all the finances in the family. After she distributed the assets, she asked for money back from me because she said she had miscalculated. I asked to see a copy of the accounts because I had never received any financial information about the estate. Her response was, 'You better not bother visiting.' I never sent the money back that she'd requested. It wasn't a lot of money, but it was the principle of the thing." Phyllis's father died seven years ago, and Phyllis and her brother haven't spoken since.

It was writing her obituary that made Phyllis think about healing the family rift. "I have a couple of friends I've known since childhood," she explains. "We get together once a month with the goal of doing something stimulating that we've never done before. One time, we decided it would be an interesting exercise to write our own obituary and then edit one another's. It was a sobering experience looking at my legacy. I could see the positives. I have been a good manager and am still in the lives of several former employees who say I had an influence on them. Also, I am part of a big extended family with many cousins, and I have a large network of friends that I spend a lot of time with. But where I have failed is in the close family department."

Phyllis does not like being estranged from her brother. "I recently had an overture from one of his daughters," she says. "So, she's provided me with an opening that I'm going to pursue. I want to rewrite that part of my legacy and undo the harm from my father's will." Phyllis's own will is very straightforward. "I have only one heir—my daughter," Phyllis says, "and she knows my financial circumstances. She will get everything, but it won't be much. I would like my friends to hold a wake for me and encourage people to give money to a particular dance organization that has meant a lot to me."

Claire is struggling with this issue of whether she should treat her children equally in her will. In her case, the dilemma comes from the fact that they have dramatically different levels of personal wealth. "Our eldest is very wealthy and our youngest is living hand to mouth," Claire explains. "So, I had a conversation with the eldest about not leaving him any money in our will. He certainly doesn't need it. But he was adamant that the estate should be equally divided in three. He promised that he and his siblings will deal with the inequities among themselves. So, our will is done this way. His reaction surprised me until I realized it's all about love, not money. His sisters live near us, but he left home as a student and never came back. He's very close to his sisters and phones them once or twice a week. He's very upset if he ever finds out that he's not in the loop. It's all about equal treatment being equated with equal love."

Although there may be good reason to treat the children equally, sometimes parents will decide to let their wills reflect their perception of the relationship. Lawyers tell me they have seen all manner of approaches. For example, a man had a falling out with his daughter. In his will, he wrote, "I am leaving $1,000 to my daughter so she can throw a party and dance on my grave." The lawyer who told me this story said, "Tempting as it might be, don't put this in your will, which becomes a public document. Write a private letter." In another instance, a woman told her lawyer she wanted to bring back into her will a son she had originally excluded. Sadly, before she could sign the papers, she was killed in a car accident. Then there was the man with three grown sons who disinherited all of them. He told his lawyer he didn't want to put any reasons in the will. "They'll know why," he said. Sometimes, people leave with the will a document that justifies differential treatment. If the will is challenged, this document could provide evidence supporting the will in the court proceedings.

In lots of families, one sibling is needier than others and may receive more financial support during the parent's lifetime. The big question becomes how to deal with this preferential treatment in the will. The amount could be considered as an advance and reflected in a reduced inheritance; or all loans and advances could be forgiven and everyone treated equally in the will. Anna's family is facing this issue, and she wants her father to be clear about his wishes.

"One of my sisters was always going to our father to ask him for money," Anna says. "Over the years, the money she has been given totalled a significant amount. It was verging on elder abuse. I asked my father to tell me honestly how he felt about what was happening. He said he was happy with the amount of money he had given my sister to date, but he didn't want to give her any more. We're now monitoring the situation closely to make sure his wishes are honoured." Anna knows her father's will as currently written divides his estate equally among the children. She is asking her father to state clearly in the will that the money given in his lifetime to this sister was given as a gift and is not to be taken into account in the division of the estate. "If this isn't made explicit," Anna says, "I'm certain there will be a battle among my siblings. It will rip the family apart."

The lawyers I interviewed said that providing evidence for your reasoning can carry weight, and it's useful to write a memo stating your thinking and to have that memo witnessed. They also recommend we let our beneficiaries know in advance what to expect in the will. But people are often reluctant to do this. A 2012 survey found that more than 60 percent of Canadians whose deceased parents had a will had never discussed the terms of the will with their parents. For those whose living parents have a will, close to 40 percent had never discussed the contents.[12]

When I interviewed Beth, she told me she wished her mother had told her brother she wouldn't be treating him equally in the will. "My brother had persistently asked my mother for money," Beth says, "so my mother decided to reduce his share of the estate. After the will's contents were revealed, my brother told us he was going to sue. We knew he would, just out of spite. So, my other brother and I both gave him money from our share just to make him go away. We knew our money would just get eaten up in legal fees anyway if it went to court. And it might even have cost us more. Mom should have talked to my brother or just treated us all equally."

Sheila was faced with the issue of unequal treatment when her mother-in-law, Abigail, asked for her advice. Abigail wanted to leave more money in her will to her son, who was Sheila's husband, than to her daughter. Sheila's husband was devoted to his mother, whereas Abigail had a difficult relationship with her daughter, which was not helped by living on different continents. Sheila had compassion for her sister-in-law. As well, she feared this unequal treatment would tear apart the family. "My sister-in-law is living a pretty hand-to-mouth existence," Sheila says. "She could certainly use the money and, more importantly, being treated differently would have broken her heart. I could see this ruining my husband's relationship with his sister. And it would destroy the positive bonds our children have with their aunt." Sheila pleaded with her mother-in-law to consider another approach that would satisfy her goal to reward her son yet keep the family peace. Sheila proposed that Abigail treat her children equally in the will while allocating monies to her two grandsons (Sheila and her husband's boys) for their education. Abigail's daughter had no children. Abigail took Sheila's suggestion and died not long after. Sheila has never shared this conversation with her family. "I don't know why Abigail decided to seek my advice, but I'm really grateful," Sheila says. "I don't think our family could have survived her unequal treatment."

Who's Your Family?

Lawyers tell me their most challenging cases involve blended families. They recommend doing everything you can to take care of the people you love. Jean is bitter that her father didn't follow this advice. Her parents divorced after thirty-seven years of marriage. Her father remarried, and Jean and her siblings never got along with his new wife. They felt their father had switched loyalties to this new spouse and her family at the expense of his own children. "After Dad married her, he was no longer my father," Jean says. "He was in his late fifties, and it was the classic case of the new wife talking the vulnerable older man into giving her all his money. Dad could have put some of his estate in trust for his children rather than leaving everything to the surviving spouse. I tried very hard to get him to change his will to do this before he died, but he didn't and she got everything. We never even got any personal items. Dad wrote in his will that an important painting was to be left to his children, and that painting has disappeared. I only wanted one piece of furniture that was part of my family heritage and I couldn't even get that. From what I've seen, what happened in Dad's case is pretty typical for second marriages. I have never really grieved Dad's death because of his treatment of us."

Wills can sometimes contain bombshells that expose secrets about who constitutes your family. Relatives may be revealed that close family didn't know existed, or relationships may be redefined. A lawyer told me about an estate she was handling in which someone's sister turned out to be her mother, and the woman she thought was her mother was actually her grandmother. The lawyer had to track down the true nature of these relationships because one of the parties had died without a will and the estate had to be distributed according to the family lineage.

Then there are stories where half-siblings emerge, either in the will or to contest the will, or as a deathbed confession. Near the end of his life, Carole's father told her in confidence that she had a half-brother he had never acknowledged. "I never told my family," Carole admits. "But when Dad died, I felt compelled to phone this man. I had no idea if he thought Dad was his father." When she called, Carole told the man that his mother's name was on a list her father had compiled. She said the list contained people her father was close to and admired, and he wanted them to be informed in the event of his death. Carole didn't reveal that he might be her half-brother, she merely asked him to tell his mother that her father had died.

"The man said that his mother was ninety-one years of age and in the hospital," she says. "It was clear that he had no knowledge of my father nor of any relationship." Carole decided that to tell him that he might be her half-brother would serve absolutely no purpose. "Even assuming my father and his mother had an affair," she says, "that didn't prove Dad was his father. And telling him about the supposed affair might destroy his relationship with his mother. So, I just let sleeping dogs lie."

A lawyer told me that in some jurisdictions, genetic material can be used after a person's death to determine these kinds of issues. So, if we have these kinds of family secrets, maybe we should face the music before our death and try to mitigate the fallout. The next section shows that trying to do the right thing can make a difference.

Can We Get It Right?

Getting our will right is not a science, and what we decide may never be perfect. But it pays to try. Helen's story illustrates how planning ahead can help ease the pain of the unimaginable. When Helen was twenty years old, she lost both her parents in a car accident. When they died, her dad was fifty-three years old and her mother was forty-eight. Helen was the middle child of six siblings ranging in age from eighteen to twenty-seven. She remembers being in shock when she heard the news. She was the only one of her siblings who refused to look at her parents' bodies in the open coffins. "A couple of my aunts and uncles said I would not be able to let my parents go if I didn't see them dead," she recalls. "My siblings didn't care whether I looked or not. They told me my parents didn't look like themselves anyway."

The accident happened nearly forty years ago and Helen remembers the funeral vividly. "We gathered in the family home," she recalls, "and everyone was there—all my brothers and sisters and my aunts and uncles. We laughed and told stories and ate. It was the best family gathering ever. We got out all my parents' old love letters and read them out loud and laughed until the tears ran down our cheeks. We sat around for three days doing this, and then they held the funeral service. We lived in a close-knit rural community, so the memorial was held in the school auditorium and hundreds of people came."

Helen was at the age and stage when it would have been easy to feel guilt-stricken about her parents' death, especially her mother's. "I worshipped my dad," she says, "and I was his favourite. I couldn't stand my mom. The last time I saw her, we had a huge fight. She had read my diary without my permission and then confronted me about my life. I got very angry with her and my last words were 'I hope I never see you again.'" Helen admits that this final argument bothered her for quite a few years. "But I felt righteous," she says. "I still think she was out of line, but I have forgiven her. She was concerned about me and wanted to know what was going on in my life."

Helen says her parents left behind lives that were in perfect order, even though their abrupt end could not have been predicted. "There was no reason for them to think they were going to die prematurely," she says. "I never remember them mentioning their deaths. They were totally healthy and from good stock. Dad came from a family of eight and Mom from a family of six, and four decades later, all of their siblings are still alive." Despite such a violent end to her parents' lives, Helen remembers the aftermath as being very orderly and comforting.

"My mother died minutes before my dad, so his will took effect," she says, "and he had appointed my mother's brother and another of his brothers-in-law as co-executors. It was my mother's brother who became the front man, and this made sense because he was a take-charge kind of guy who got things done. After the funeral, he sat us siblings down to explain the process. We all wanted to get on with our lives and return to what we had been doing before our parents' death. The will had been structured to provide financial support to allow that to happen. It took about three years to settle the estate, but my uncle had a good idea of how much we each would be receiving. So, during that period, we borrowed against that amount as needed."

Helen remembers the dividing up of assets as being remarkably free of drama. "The only asset of any value was some property," she says. "There was a car, piano, sewing machine and antique table, and the rest was standard furniture, dishes, pots and pans. There were personal mementos, but no precious items and no art. Our uncle had determined an approximate value for each item and we were asked to identify what single item was most important to us. None of us picked the same thing. We then went around in a circle from youngest to oldest choosing among the remaining items. The objective was that we would each have the same monetary value for what we chose, and any imbalance would be resolved through the final financial settlement. All of us felt that what was decided was fair. Everybody wanted the best for everybody else. Nothing was left unresolved. To this day, we all say, 'How come that was so easy?'"

Helen's summation of this experience is a remarkable testament to her parents' legacy. What she describes is not merely the result of good estate planning; it also illustrates the outcome of lives well lived. "Immediately after my parents died," Helen says, "none of us said that we no longer had a home, although that was true in one sense. For us, our home was the family that was left, and the memories. We talked about all the camping trips, how our parents made us take music lessons, how hard we worked all the time, and how we had a really cool family. We all liked each other and we got on with our lives."

It helped that the children felt their parents had lived full, rich lives. "When my parents died, they didn't have a care in the world," Helen says. "They were so in love with one another. They were so happy. Even if they had known they were going to die, I don't believe they would have done anything differently. We kept saying, 'They've had such a good life.'"

What Helen learned from her parents is playing out in her life. "I've always had a will," she says, "and it's always up to date, and I have life insurance. I don't want to leave my children in the lurch, having to sell assets to make payments. I am trying to leave nothing in an unfinished state, even stuff like their photo albums. I don't hold on to junk. I try to deal with my stuff, clothes, shoes, knick-knacks, even paper. I'm trying to simplify my life. I don't want to leave the mess for my kids. The thought of dying never bothers me. I have told everyone I love that I love them, and there is nothing left unsaid or left undone."

When it came to my dear friend KS, she too left nothing unsaid or undone. I was astonished to learn she had rewritten her will just a few months before she was killed. Enclosed with her will was a four-page handwritten letter addressed to her sons to be given to them on the event of her death. Her letter begins with an expression of love for them and goes on to explain in detail the thought process that went into resolving the practical matters of "what to do with my estate now that I have a partner."

The letter begins, "What I want to say to you first is something that you already know. I love you both with all my heart." She wrote that she had been totally unprepared for the joy and love her sons brought into her life. She knew "the love that I feel for you cannot and will not die . . . and will surround you both all your lives." The letter explains that she and her partner intended that their own children would be the major beneficiaries of each of their estates, and they had made provision for one another largely through designation of their RRSPs and insurance policies.

KS wrote that she was leaving the house (which she owned) to them as part of her estate and that she wanted it to be their home for as long as they wished. At the time, her sixteen-year-old son was living at home and the nineteen-year-old was away at university. Her partner was also living in the house. KS wrote, "I don't want him to be dispossessed, particularly at a time at which he will be very vulnerable." She asked her sons to be sensitive to his needs when they were deciding what to do with the house, and the letter set out some possible scenarios. She concluded, "I did think it was important to let you know what my thoughts were; however, I trust you both to arrive at a good decision that will respect everyone's needs, given my love for all three of you." She signed it, "Yours always."

On so many levels, KS has given us a textbook case of what the lawyers recommend: revisit your will if circumstances change, articulate your thinking so your loved ones understand your thought process, and be thoughtful about the impact on those you love. KS and her partner had been living together in her home for several months and were talking marriage, so this precipitated the rewriting of the will. And the care and consideration she demonstrated for her loved ones set a high standard for us all. As for the timing, it was providential—even smacking of divine foresight. Fifty-one days after KS signed those documents, she was dead and her boys were reading her letter. When I asked her son about that experience, he said, "It was eerie to hear her from beyond the grave like that. I'm certainly glad she wrote the letter, although it was thankfully a bit unnecessary—that is, most of it didn't need saying." But KS was never one to leave things to chance.

One of the very important decisions we make when we draw up our will is to appoint an executor. As the stories in the next chapter illustrate, the role of the executor is critical to ensuring our wishes are honoured. The job can have its challenges and we need to choose someone who is up to the task.

The Dubious Honour

The person we name as our executor has the job of carrying out our wishes as expressed in our will. Lawyers refer to this job as a "dubious honour"—for good reason. The specific duties comprise a list as long as your arm, including making our funeral arrangements; finding, valuing and liquidating our assets; handling our liabilities; paying our outstanding bills; filing for probate (the official proving of the will), if required; and paying our taxes. I have been the executor of three estates and I can confirm that this is a job that needs to be taken seriously. The executor can make mistakes and be sued, is legally responsible for unpaid taxes, and needs to comply with pretty demanding legal rules for record-keeping. But you don't need to do this all by yourself. Each time I was the executor, I had significant assistance as needed from lawyers, accountants and financial advisers. However, in the final analysis, the buck stopped with me.

As you can see from their duties, the executors we choose need to be comfortable with legal and financial issues, and they need research skills to ferret out all the pertinent information relevant to our estate. But equally important, and harder to quantify, are the qualities executors require for handling the emotional fallout from our death. Our hope is that they will execute all these responsibilities in a way that would make us happy. The executor is acting as our agent, and even though we'll be dead, we want to leave people with that warm glow we were talking about earlier. Given that the executor is one of the main curators of our afterlife, we need to make that appointment with great care.

Lawyers recommend we appoint an executor who's younger than us, so they're still alive and "fit for service" when we die. We can appoint more than one executor to share the task, but the more executors, the longer decisions will take. Also, we should designate an alternate, in the event that our first choice for executor is unable or unwilling to do the job. It's easier if our executor lives in the same country as we do, but the ease of communicating digitally means they don't need to live near our lawyer or our financial institutions to do a good job.

We need to talk to our designated executor in advance. You don't want this to be a surprise. After our death, he is free to turn down the assignment, even if he agreed to it previously. Circumstances change, and this is why we need to appoint an alternate. What we don't want is someone starting the process and giving up partway through. You can imagine the problems that would ensue. The executor can receive payment for the job—usually a percentage based on the size of the estate. If we decide instead to engage a professional executor, we should make an agreement with her in advance to establish a fee structure.

Whom Should We Choose as Executor?

Lawyers have seen it all when it comes to choosing executors and ask us to try and face reality when making this decision. "Some people want to name all their children as executors," one lawyer says, "but they're ignoring the fact that the children don't get along. I had a case where five of the seven children were executors, and it was impossible to get a decision. Sometimes, choosing one child does put the noses of the other children out of joint, and they can make life difficult for the executor. But you have to set these considerations aside and choose the right person for the job. One way to avoid fights is to appoint a professional executor."

Kathy has been the executor of two estates and feels that if people are honest, there is one person in every family who is the right choice to be executor. "They need to be smart enough to understand the process," she says, "and they have to be a peacemaker. They need to be firm but fair. Many families have siblings that don't get along, and the executor must never penalize the sibling they don't like. He needs to have integrity and protect the wounded members of the family. When you make your will, you should discuss your choice of executor with everyone so there are no surprises. Or you could hire a professional executor. The only downside is that it will cost more money."

Kathy was the sole executor of the first estate she handled and things went smoothly. "It took me about a year to wrap everything up," she says, "including filing the final tax returns. Each task took a lot of time—organizing the funeral, cashing insurance cheques, getting probate, et cetera."

The next time Kathy was appointed executor, it was for her mother's estate, and this time she was co-executor along with her brother. "This process was way more challenging," she says. "Mom chose to add my brother because she loved him and didn't want to hurt his feelings. When things started out, he was doing nothing and I was doing everything, and I became resentful. So, I assigned him certain tasks. Then I started keeping track of my hours and asked him to submit his hours for work he'd done. After that, if I assigned him a job, he took it on, but there was no independent effort on his part. However, he wrote a beautiful obituary. Overall, it worked out. I was happy for him and I liked having someone to discuss things with."

Blended families, in particular, often struggle with the question of whom to designate as executor. Chris and Elizabeth have been married for decades. Chris is significantly older than Elizabeth and is in poor health, so they anticipate he will predecease her. They didn't have children together, and Elizabeth feels that Chris's children have never completely warmed to her, even after all these years. When Chris suggested appointing one of his children as executor for his will, Elizabeth was adamant they needed a neutral third party. "Your will can't anticipate every circumstance," she said to Chris, "and I don't trust your children to act in my best interest, even though that is your intention." Although Chris doesn't share Elizabeth's fears that she wouldn't be treated fairly by his children, he has agreed to respect her wishes. They have appointed a friend of theirs to be the executor of both their estates. This woman is younger than them and a former lawyer. "You have to trust that your executor will carry out your wishes, not substitute their own," Elizabeth says.

Similarly, Carole and Malcolm have no joint children. However, in their case, they both have children of their own. When I asked Malcolm whom he was going to appoint as executor of his will, he named three people: his wife, a mutual friend who is a lawyer, and his youngest daughter. Malcolm has four children and said he was conflicted about singling out this one daughter. "This will be difficult for the senior daughter to accept because she thinks she's in charge of our family," he says. "My son's nose will also be out of joint. Both of them dislike this youngest sister and don't always trust her. But the oldest has no interest in financial matters and the next oldest is such a procrastinator. Ultimately, my wife will have to deal with this. Happily, she feels close to the children and makes a big effort to maintain a good relationship with them. She will work very hard to make everything work out."

Given his ambivalence, I ask Malcolm why he feels the need to include his daughter as one of the executors. He says, "I admit we're really struggling with this. We thought it would appease my children. We thought they would see my daughter as protecting her side of the family and her siblings' interests. But I know their solidarity can't be assumed. After my first wife died, one of my children went around the condo and pocketed everything that was coloured silver. As for including our friend as executor, we thought we shouldn't have just family members. This way, the family executors could seek advice from someone outside the family. Another option would be for us to have a professional executor. We're reviewing our wills every two to five years, so although my will is written this way now, it may change."

When legal advisers hear these kinds of stories, they stress the importance of talking to the parties in advance of any decision about designating executors. "You need to talk to the proposed executors and assess their capability and their willingness. And you need to talk to those who may have expected to be executors so they understand your reasoning and your decision doesn't come as a shock," an adviser cautioned. My aunt followed this advice when designating my father as her executor, with me as a backup. When my aunt discussed this with us, she was in her seventies and she wasn't the picture of health. My father was seven years younger and very fit. Financial matters were his specialty and it was assumed that he would be the one handling her estate. But by the time my aunt died at nearly ninety years of age, Dad was eight-four and had neither the capacity nor the energy for the task. However, he was reluctant to pass the responsibility on to me, feeling he was reneging on his duty. As well, he thought this unexpected burden would come as a surprise to me. Fortunately, I was able to remind him of our conversation with my aunt. He realized I had been fully informed and prepared, which eased his considerable feelings of guilt.

How Much Discretion for Our Executor?

Some wills provide broad direction and permit, even require, executors to exercise significant discretion in their implementation. Other wills set out specific directives that allow executors limited flexibility. The two stories you'll read next stand in sharp contrast to one another. In the first instance, a professional executor did not feel he had the authority to give a relative a small memento from his deceased client's estate. In the second case, the executor was given a complicated assignment that entailed using some of her mother's estate to try and repair ruptured family ties.

In the first example, the will belonged to Grant, who at age sixty-five suffered a major stroke. Seven years later, he died from the after-effects of the stroke coupled with a bout of cancer. Grant had always lived alone, and his parents and siblings had predeceased him. But he had a devoted circle of relatives and friends, and when he became ill, several of them formed a care team. Grant had given power of attorney for finance and health care to his lawyer, but over the seven years of Grant's incapacity, there were a myriad of jobs that required the dedicated involvement of his circle of care.

During the first year after his stroke, Grant's condition slowly improved, and he was moved from the hospital to a rehab centre, and then to a facility with modified assisted living. Through these relocations, members of Grant's care team visited him, supported him and facilitated the moves. They made sure that someone was present at his numerous medical meetings to ask questions and be his advocate. When it became clear that Grant would never be able to live on his own, the team helped clear out his house and prepare it for sale. The proceeds from the sale were sufficient to finance his move to a retirement home, and team members presented him with his housing options and then helped him move in.

Patricia is Grant's cousin and was a dedicated member of his care team. "Grant was witty and loved to laugh, and he loved to talk," she recalls. "He was frustrated that he couldn't get back to his old self after the stroke. He worked hard at his therapy and definitely improved over the years, but eventually they told him that his speech would likely not improve any more." People from Grant's circle of care visited as often as they could to keep his spirits up and bring him the latest gossip. "He was passionate about politics and history," says Patricia, "and he loved being kept in the loop. He had been a loyal and generous friend, and we were happy to be there for him."

After Grant's death, the care team organized his memorial, wrote the obituary and participated in the burial decisions. Some weeks after the funeral, Patricia realized that she didn't have a single item to remind her of her cousin. She wrote to the lawyer who was Grant's executor. "I knew he was settling up the estate," she recalls, "and in my letter, I asked if I could be given a small remembrance of Grant's, something that had belonged to him—a book, for example." She received a terse reply from the lawyer saying that Grant had not made provisions for this in his will, so it would not be possible to grant her request.

"I was completely taken aback and deeply hurt by this response," Patricia says. "The lawyer was a man I had come to know well through the years of working together to support Grant, and his reply was very uncaring. But, more importantly, I felt bereft at being denied a single item to connect me with Grant. We had transferred his small collection of books and art and mementos from location to location to make it more homelike. At any point, I could easily have asked Grant for a small keepsake and he would have happily complied. But I could never bring myself to do that; it would have been such an acknowledgement that he was dying. Anything I wanted would have had absolutely no monetary value—one of his history books or a photo of his parents. I am left with such sad, unresolved feelings. I know that Grant would be upset at this outcome. This is not what he would have wanted."

We assume that Grant's lawyer was acting according to the will. This case reminds us, when drafting our will, to try and put ourselves in the shoes of those who care about us and will be left behind when we depart. It's easy to think of our will as a legal document that tidies up our estate while ignoring the fact that it is our last communication with our loved ones.

In sharp contrast to the case above, Kathy's mother gave a great deal of thought to what would happen to her family after her death, and she wanted to make a difference, even from the grave. She decided to use some of her estate to try and repair fractured family relationships and entrusted her daughter as executor to make it happen.

Kathy has three brothers, and all four siblings have children of their own. Kathy's mother was estranged from two of her sons, and the siblings had difficult relationships with one another as well. Kathy's mother hoped that the next generation, her grandchildren, would be able to rise above this family legacy and form their own relationships with one another. With this goal in mind, she stipulated in her will that money be set aside to throw a party once a year for all her grandchildren. "She set aside five thousand dollars per year to cover the party costs and airfare for the grandchildren who had to fly," says Kathy. "She wrote this into her will without understanding the legal requirements, and she wasn't well served by her lawyer. Since the children were under eighteen years of age, I had to set up a children's trust and work within the children's trust laws to get it approved. It was a real nightmare."

Kathy admits that the whole thing has been a burden but says she has to give her mother credit. "Something really good has come from this," Kathy says. "At the party, I met, for the first time, the two sons of one of my brothers, and they turned out to be really outstanding young men. When the older one decided to go to a university near us, he asked if he could live with my family. We agreed, and we were able to find him a part-time job to help him with his finances. He plans to complete his entire university degree in two years. It's been an amazing adventure for him. This was my mother's gift."

But Kathy has found it challenging to carry out her mother's wishes. "If I can't get the party together every year, I let it lapse," she says. "I know it was my mother's way of trying to keep the family together after her death, and I respect her wishes. But if our siblings don't grow in the same way we do, we don't need to feel bad that we're not best friends."

Talking with all these people about their experiences and having been an executor myself, I'm further persuaded of the importance of selecting someone with extraordinarily good judgment as your executor. In exercising her duty, the executor will need to protect our legacy in circumstances we couldn't possibly foresee. The next three stories show this principle in action. You'll read about how people's legacies have been either protected and enhanced or damaged and diminished by decisions made by their executors.

Franz Kafka's Legacy

As I was thinking about the complex decisions required in being a good executor, I remembered hearing about the case of Franz Kafka. Evidently, the renowned writer had directed that all his work be burned after his death. Clearly, his literary executor had ignored his instructions in a decision worth applauding. We would be impoverished without Kafka's literary masterpieces and would have been deprived of the evocative adjective that has emerged from his writing. Describing something as "Kafkaesque" vividly calls forth the illogical, menacing atmosphere of *The Trial*, or the bizarre, claustrophobic world of *The Metamorphosis*.

Kafka was a German-speaking Jewish writer who was born in Prague in 1883 and died from tuberculosis at the age of forty. In his day job, he worked as an assessor of insurance claims, and his writing was relegated to his spare time. Although Kafka wrote copiously, including short stories, diaries, and letters to family and friends, very little was published in his lifetime. In 1902, Kafka met Max Brod, the man who was to become his close friend, literary executor and cheerleader. Brod declared, "All Franz Kafka's utterances about life were profound and original." Brod also became Kafka's literary arm-wrestler. "I wrested from Kafka nearly everything he published either by persuasion or by guile," he wrote.[1]

Kafka did not leave behind a will. However, among a mass of papers on his desk was a note addressed to Brod in which he outlined his "last request." His instructions were explicit: "Everything I leave behind me (in my bookcase, linen-cupboard, and my desk both at home and in the office, or anywhere else where anything may have got to and meets your eye), in the way of diaries, manuscripts, letters (my own and others'), sketches, and so on, to be burned unread."[2] He also wanted Brod to gather and burn any of his writings and sketches that other people had, including anything Brod himself possessed. If people chose not to surrender this material to Brod, Kafka wanted them to promise to burn it themselves.

Despite this direction, a year after Kafka's death, Brod published *The Trial*. The publication contained a postscript in which Brod reprinted Kafka's "categorical instructions" (see page 156) and defended his decision to "refuse to perform the holocaust demanded of me by my friend."[3] Brod wrote that Kafka had a negative attitude toward his work because he was a perfectionist, motivated by standards that were too high, and in addition, unhappy experiences drove him to self-sabotage. Brod claimed that nonetheless, Kafka took real pleasure from seeing his books in print. Brod's "chief defence" for ignoring Kafka's instructions was that he had told his friend he would not comply with them. When Kafka had shown him the folded note, telling him it was his last testament containing the request that he burn everything, Brod replied, "If you seriously think me capable of such a thing, let me tell you here and now that I shall not carry out your wishes."[4] Brod wrote that Kafka should have appointed another executor if he wanted his instructions to stand.

Brod continued to publicly release Kafka's writings, including the first complete edition of his works, published by Schocken Verlag beginning in 1935. Kafka's biographer Reiner Stach says that Brod brought Kafka's works to publication as quickly and completely as possible, but he didn't always preserve the manuscripts in their original condition. "He had no scruples about making his own annotations and cuts to the manuscripts (some of which he himself had rescued), sending originals by mail even before they had been deciphered, or giving away individual pages as gifts," says Stach.[5] But Brod was a passionate collector of Kafka's every creative output, and it is thanks to him that readers and scholars have so much memorabilia to explore. He even saved some of Kafka's attempts at drawing and preserved the scribbles in the margins of his lecture notes.

As to the question of whether Kafka should have entrusted Brod with such a strict act of destruction if he had not meant it seriously, Stach argues that the reality is that no one besides Brod even had access to the papers designated for destruction. "Brod became the executor of Kafka's will because no one else could have executed this will," he says. However, Stach points out that Kafka burned some material himself, so he may have known that Brod would not follow his instructions.[6] In the final analysis, the overwhelming majority of critics and readers have approved of Brod's decision.

Taking Kafka's instructions at face value, we could assume he wanted to dwindle into obscurity, little known beyond his narrow circle in Prague and Vienna. Yet Kafka chose to leave his long-term interests in the hands of someone who believed in his genius and who was unlikely to support any aspirations that he fade away. As a result, his books have been adapted to every medium, his work has been the subject of countless treatises, and the adjective *Kafkaesque* is connected with inhumanity and absurdity in more than one hundred languages.[7] As in this case, an executor may decide to ignore your wishes for the greater good.

My own experience has given me some insight into Brod's dilemma. Some years ago, a friend we'll call Virginia, a celebrated academic, asked if we could meet about a matter of some importance to her. We were very close friends and, although we lived in different cities, we managed to spend a great deal of time together. She came to visit, and after we sat down, she got right to the point. She was in the process of revising her will and intended to assign me a specific task, and she wanted my permission. Her intention was to place her personal correspondence in a folder with my name on it and marked "Destroy without Reading." In the event of her death, her executor would deliver the package to me to carry out her wishes.

Virginia thought the process was a mere formality and expected me to quickly agree. But we sat in silence for some long minutes while I pondered the request. Then I told Virginia I had to say no. She was taken aback and responded, "But you're the only one of my friends I could trust to do this without reading anything." I replied, "I could easily say yes now, but I have to be honest with you. When the time came to carry out the destruction, I don't believe I could do it." As I explained to Virginia, her career had been groundbreaking and I hoped, in years to come, she would be heralded for her accomplishments. I envisioned her becoming the subject of extensive research resulting in biographies and academic papers, and I told her I could not imagine myself destroying material that might contribute to this process.

Before Virginia and I switched topics, I asked whether she was ill and had reason to anticipate needing her will. Fortunately, she affirmed that she was healthy, and I got to enjoy her company for many more years. When she did die, it was after a prolonged battle with cancer. Unlike the abrupt death she was anticipating, her illness gave her the time she needed to put her affairs in order to her own satisfaction. Although Virginia and I didn't discuss the topic again, she probably got rid of the contents of her "Destroy without Reading" file herself. My experience with Virginia gives me confidence that Brod did the right thing. Kafka, too, suffered a lengthy illness and had plenty of opportunity to destroy his own material. Whatever he left behind, part of him must have wanted us to see.

The next story, about how Janice exercised her responsibilities for William's estate, provides a contemporary example of the complexities of the executor's task and how your legacy will benefit if your executor is up to the challenge.

William's Legacy

When William was introduced to Janice by a mutual friend in a café, little did he know that he would die without warning and that Janice would become the literary executor for his estate. He also could not have imagined that Janice would dedicate a goodly amount of her energy, time and resources to developing and promoting his legacy.

When William and Janice met, they were both in their fifties and their lives had uncanny overlaps. "We had worked for the same company," Janice says, "although not at the same time. We'd even sat in the same little cubbyhole. We'd grown up in the same town and gone to the same dancing school. We were both English Lang and Lit grads. We had a shared sense of humour and view of the world." The bonds of friendship deepened when William decided to write a novel and Janice offered to read his drafts. The process went on for years as the book went through three revisions. "He genuinely welcomed my input," Janice recalls, "and it was a real pleasure for the two of us to discuss the writing style, the plot development, and the ideas that he was trying to express."

Through the intimacy of the editorial process, they got to know and trust one another. Janice suggested William give her power of attorney for his personal care. "William was an only child," she explains. "His parents had died and he didn't have any close relatives. I wanted to be able to advocate for him should he ever be hospitalized. My husband and I had watched a single man we knew very well needing extra assistance in the hospital, so we'd seen what could happen. I wanted to be able to do this for William, if needed." When he turned sixty-nine, William got around to visiting his lawyer and making this arrangement. "I was relieved when he told me," Janice says. "But then he laughed and told me that he had also made me his literary executor. Perhaps every author expects glory, and I think William thought he would be leaving me a financial treasure as well as a literary one. The responsibilities didn't weigh heavily on me at the time. Neither of us expected him to die in the foreseeable future."

But a few months later, William was dead. "He died very suddenly," Janice recalls. "I had coffee with him on Saturday morning, and on Sunday he went to the hospital with abdominal pain." He died several days later from post-surgery complications. After Janice organized the memorial service and oversaw the burial arrangements, she began to grasp the full extent of the commitment she'd made to William. "His will was rather general," Janice says, "and I think if he had thought he was actually going to die, rather than just going through a formality, he would have been more specific. He appointed a trust company as financial executor and we had to work together. I had an ongoing dialogue with the person assigned and he tried to be accommodating, but the approach was costly and restrictive, and there were tensions."

Janice discovered there were many aspects to her role as literary executor, but getting William's book published became a priority for her. "William had tried unsuccessfully to find an agent and a publisher," she says, "and for him, the book became all about having his voice heard in the world. A difficult childhood had left him struggling with a lack of self-confidence, and I felt the book's publication would complete a part of William's journey. I considered the book to be his most cherished project, so I treated this as my top priority. When it was finally published, I felt it was the best legacy he could have."

But Janice's responsibilities didn't end there. A major part of William's legacy had to do with his impressive art collection, which he had willed to two major museums. The art had to be appraised, crated and shipped, and Janice supervised it all. "Some very large wooden sculptures had to be very carefully packed for shipping," she recalls. "This was a complicated and costly procedure. One sculpture was so large, it had to come out through a second-storey balcony as it could not go down the stairs. It was complicated dealing with the other effects in his home because nothing could be done until all the valuable art had been removed."

The art donation took on a new dimension when a curator decided to use William's collection as the inspiration for an exhibit that showcased the art, the artists and their cultural origins. Janice obtained the funding for the exhibition catalogue and brought people to the exhibition opening. "There were hundreds of people there," she recalls, "and the curator's notes gave William great credit. He would have been so satisfied that his art collection was 'at work,' giving people pleasure, information, and leading to future developments."

And Janice kept going. She came up with another memorial for William, one that had never crossed his mind. "I suggested to William's friends that we make a donation to renovate the quiet room in the hospital's intensive care unit," she says. "This is the unit where William spent his last days, and the quiet room is where medical staff deliver the news to people about their loved ones, sometimes bad news. The room was extremely unattractive and didn't have a comforting or meditative quality. This project took a long time to complete, but the hospital was very grateful and included me in their planning. Finally, this year, a much lovelier room will become part of William's legacy."

When William chose Janice as his executor, he identified someone with both the wherewithal and the commitment to expend an enormous amount of time and effort to act in the interest of his legacy. She had the specialized skills and expertise to handle the book publication and the art donations. In addition, Janice had the advantage of knowing William's values and his dreams. In all her dealings, she was acting as his proxy, so she needed to know his thinking.

There is another aspect of being an executor that is well illustrated by their story. In cases where our executor will benefit financially from our estate, we hope they will weigh the needs of our legacy fairly alongside their personal gains. Janice inherited the balance of the estate proceeds. She chose to allocate a significant amount of money to realizing William's legacy, and many of these decisions were completely at her discretion. "There were no specific amounts of money allocated," Janice explains, "neither for the book nor the art collection. William knew how committed I was to the book, and probably was sure I would do the right thing, whatever that was. He fully expected the book to make money, which is probably unrealistic. Also, he didn't think about adding any money for the museums to care for the art. They didn't even have the money for the exhibition catalogue, so I paid for most of that."

I asked Janice how William would feel about the job she has done. "I have felt William looking over my shoulder," she says, "and he is taking pleasure in how his projects are going. He would have loved the exhibit of his art at the museum, he would have been thrilled with his book, and he would have delighted in some of the uses I have made of his money."

I ask Janice, based on her experience, what advice she would have given William about his will. "The real problem was that William did not go into this actually thinking he might die," she says. "He wanted me to be his attorney for personal care, and that's why he went to see a lawyer. It was his lawyer who suggested he should also do a will. I believe she wanted him to come back and go over things, but he didn't want to. He didn't want to think about his death, and a will is about your death and dealing with things after your death."

Janice thinks that if William had gone back to his lawyer, she would have helped him be more detailed about his art. "William told me he had made a list of the specific art pieces to be donated," she says. "We never found that list, so we had to use general categories. William's will didn't specify gifts or mementos for friends, so I tried to do this as best I could. However, even small items that fell into the broad art categories could not be kept out of the museum donations. I think William would have wanted to leave some things to friends. Had he known he was going to die, I believe there are other things he would have done."

Carrying out her role as literary executor has taken Janice years. She knows she has done an exemplary job. "Not everyone would be willing to care for these works of art the way I have cared for them," she admits. "But I didn't find it hard to make the effort required to realize William's dream. He was gentle and fierce, elegant and fine, and deeply touched the lives of those he cared about."

The stories of Kafka and William illustrate how an executor can protect, even enhance, the legacy of the deceased. The case of Andy Warhol shows the flip side of the coin. When it came time to settle the estate of the legendary artist and filmmaker, one might well assume, given all his wealth and fame, he would have been able to secure a similar outcome. Not so, as you'll read next.

Andy Warhol's Legacy

In 1987, Warhol died suddenly at age fifty-eight, leaving an estate estimated by the courts to be over $500 million in value.[8] He directed in his will that the bulk of this estate be used to establish a foundation for visual arts. Warhol's biographer Paul Alexander argues in his 1994 book *Death and Disaster: The Rise of the Warhol Empire and the Race for Andy's Millions* that the foundation, which should have secured his legacy, tried to discredit his reputation as an artist, and that battles between the estate and the foundation drained resources away from organizations and artists that should have benefitted from his estate.

Warhol played a prominent role in the artistic revolution of the 1960s. The art critic Arthur Danto argues that beyond creating innovative art, Warhol changed the very concept of art itself. Danto wrote, "His work induced a transformation in art's philosophy so deep that it was no longer possible to think of art in the same way that it had been thought of even a few years before him."[9] Reading this, I was reminded of seeing Lily Tomlin on stage holding two identical Warhol graphics of a Campbell's tomato soup can. Tomlin was starring in the Broadway production of *The Search for Signs of Intelligent Life in the Universe* and was trying to explain life on earth to extraterrestrials, her "space chums." She points to one image, calling it "soup," and then points to its twin, calling it "art." She sums up the aliens' problem: "They find it hard to grasp some things that come easy to us, because they simply don't have our frame of reference."[10]

Whereas Warhol may have philosophically changed art history in the 1960s, critics argue that the latter period of his life did not have the same artistic impact. The year 1968 is noted as the turning point. In June, Warhol was shot in his office by a rejected hanger-on, leaving him clinically dead. He was brought back to life on the operating table by open heart massage. The shooting changed Warhol. He told a reporter, "Since I was shot, everything is such a dream to me. I don't know whether or not I'm really alive—whether I died . . . And having died once, I shouldn't feel fear. But I'm afraid."[11]

The change in Warhol's life coincided with his decision to revise his role from "artist" to "artist-executive" in charge of "art business." Warhol described this new focus in his book *The Philosophy of Andy Warhol: From A to B and Back Again.* He explains that he had started out as a commercial artist, and he wanted to finish as a business artist. "Being good in business is the most fascinating kind of art . . . making money is art and working is art, and good business is the best art."[12] To this end, in 1971, Warhol established Andy Warhol Enterprises, Inc., and proved himself an astute businessman, intimately involved in all aspects of his expanding empire. One of his employees recalled, "All our lawyers and business advisers were always amazed at how good Andy was at really understanding the basic concepts of a deal. There was no question that he knew what he wanted."[13]

Sixteen years later, Warhol died, and this second death was just as unexpected as the first. He went into hospital for a routine removal of an infected gallbladder and died from complications. But Warhol was prepared and left behind a will that clearly articulated his wishes. Aside from bequests to a few named individuals, the rest of his estate was to go to a "Foundation for the Visual Arts." He specified that the foundation be established as a charitable organization. The will designated as the executor a man who had been his key adviser for twenty years, and this man was also to serve on the foundation board of directors. Warhol left it to the board to name the foundation and write its statement of purpose. The board determined that the Andy Warhol Foundation for the Visual Arts would support and award grants to cultural institutions and organizations in the United States and abroad.

Warhol's half-a-billion-dollar estate was enormous in terms of size and complexity, containing investments, real estate, collectibles and the largest asset—his art collection, which was second in size only to Picasso's. In *Death and Disaster*,

Paul Alexander argues that things went wrong with Warhol's legacy when the foundation's board appointed a director who had no experience running a foundation with assets to be managed, and who didn't know anything about art or the business of art, or the artist himself. "He didn't even seem to *like* Warhol—his art, his films, the person he was, what he stood for."[14] By 1990, the estate and the foundation were involved in bitter conflicts that ended up in court. Alexander says one of the underlying issues was that the foundation accepted low-end appraisal evaluations of Warhol's work. This strategy reduced the amount of money the organization was obligated to distribute to the public as a charity, since maintaining its charitable status required the foundation to give away annually 5 percent of the balance of the estate.

As a result, the foundation was in the surprising position of using Warhol's own money to undermine his legacy. Alexander describes an exchange in court when the foundation's own attorney was trying to destroy Warhol's reputation as an artist. "She was determined to prove . . . that Warhol's art was a fad, that it was declining in value *at this very moment*, and that as a result it was a bad investment."[15] The battles drained millions from the foundation's capacity to support artists and their art.

This all happened several decades ago. The foundation's twenty-year report (1987–2007) divided its major achievements into two categories: its ongoing efforts to secure Warhol's legacy, and its role as the pre-eminent national funder of innovative contemporary art.[16] This seems more like what Warhol had in mind.

Revisiting Our Choice of Executor

We need to keep revisiting our will and re-examining our choice of executor because things change. The point is well illustrated by Eliza's story. Eliza married into a close-knit family. Her husband's five siblings were married and, over the years, all the couples had children. At the outset, their wills took similar approaches. In the event of one spouse dying, the partner would be the executor. If they both died, one or more of their siblings, or their siblings' spouses, would be executors. As time passed and the offspring became adults themselves, the siblings decided that it was appropriate for people to name their own children as executors.

Eliza and her husband, Ben, were in agreement with the plan. "When this approach was being discussed, I realized we hadn't looked at our wills for a long time," Eliza remembers. "I was at the bank and decided to get the will out of our safety deposit box to refresh my memory. What I read terrified me. If both Ben and I were to die, we had named Jo, my brother-in-law, to be the executor." Eliza was upset because some years previously, Jo and his wife had divorced. The acrimonious process had created a permanent rupture, and Jo no longer spoke to anyone in Eliza's extended family. Jo had remarried and moved away, and neither Eliza nor Ben had seen him in years. "Even worse," Eliza said, "Jo had some serious mental health issues and I wouldn't trust his judgment for a minute—especially when it came to our family."

Eliza called her husband in a panic and told him he had to leave work immediately and together they would figure out what to do. As Eliza recalls, "Ben laughed and reminded me that Jo's role only came into effect if we both died. So, it would be best if we stayed apart until the whole thing got resolved." Eliza called their lawyer and insisted he write them new wills right away. "He told me nicely to calm down," she remembers, "and suggested I go to a website he recommended and download and complete a simple form. This would override the current will and solve my immediate problem. He scheduled an appointment with us for the following week, when we would have the time to carefully think through our wishes, and he would revise the wills. It's all resolved now. But it was a close call and a good lesson about keeping our wills up to date!"

In the next section, we look at giving back. Most of us don't like to think that when we die, the world will not be any different than it would have been if we had never lived. If we focus only on ourselves, our permanent extinction is probably guaranteed. We donate time and money while we're alive because we want to see the immediate benefits for our community and our world, and we hope to have some long-lasting impact after we're gone. In addition, by giving now, we can gain insight into the effectiveness of the organizations we're supporting and make decisions about legacy giving in our wills. The next chapter explores various experiences that people have with giving back and what we can learn from them.

Giving Back

When I ask people about their legacy, their activities with charitable and non-profit organizations figure large. The vast majority of us donate our money and many of us volunteer our time, and we have seen the difference one person can make.[1] Terry Fox is an example of legacy at its finest. Most of us have seen an image of this extraordinary young man as he struggled to complete his cross-Canada run in 1980 to raise money and awareness for cancer research. He was twenty-two years old and running on an artificial limb attached to the stump of his right leg. He had lost the leg to cancer when he was eighteen. He called his run the Marathon of Hope. He managed to make it more than halfway across Canada before the cancer spread from his legs to his lung, and he had to return home for more treatment. He died ten months later. Fox may have lost his battle with cancer, but his achievements exceeded even his soaring ambition. He had asked every Canadian to donate one dollar to his cause in order to raise $22 million, which at the time seemed like an impossible dream for this unknown young man with a tiny support team. By the thirty-fifth anniversary of his run, the foundation in his name had raised $700 million.

Fox received countless awards that cemented his legacy—he was the youngest Companion of the Order of Canada, his portrait hangs in Canada's Sports Hall of Fame, and a mountain was named after him in his home province of British Columbia. But these towering achievements have been overshadowed by his most impactful legacy: the millions who have taken up his mantle to support his cause. Every year, in over nine thousand communities across Canada, and in some sixty countries around the world, hundreds of thousands of people participate in Terry Fox runs to keep his dream alive. And then there are the countless others who have been inspired by his example to start initiatives for their own cause.

Terry Fox's quest was infused with his passion and this is one of the reasons he touches our hearts. While undergoing chemotherapy, he was overcome by the pain and despair that surrounded him in the treatment rooms, and he became determined to take himself to the limit to try and help alleviate the suffering. "Somewhere the hurting must stop," he wrote in his letter requesting support for his run. "We need your help. The people in cancer clinics all over the world need people who believe in miracles."[2]

When we think we can't make a difference to the world because of our financial or personal limitations, it behooves us to consider Terry Fox. His accomplishment in the face of seemingly insurmountable odds challenges us and our rationalizations. Fox maintained that he was not special. "I just wish people would realize that anything's possible, if you try; dreams are made, if people try."[3] Although Fox's achievements may be beyond us, his strategy of asking each of us to donate one dollar reminds us that we all have the capacity to make a contribution. His legacy is a testament to the power of giving what we can.

Tracy Gary is a non-profit entrepreneur and legacy adviser who wrote *Inspired Philanthropy* to improve people's lifetime giving. Gary is clear that philanthropy is not just for the wealthy. The word, derived from the Greek, means "love of humankind," and Gary describes philanthropy as giving time, talent or treasure for the public good. She insists that those who donate twenty-five dollars to a nursery school raffle have earned the right to call themselves philanthropists.

Gary says that it was considering her will and the bequest she would be making that got her thinking about her current giving. "Then I thought, if I'm planning my giving for when I'm dead," she writes, "what's stopping me from doing it now? That's when I decided to use my will as a blueprint for a yearly giving plan."[4] She argues that everyone benefits if we integrate our values, passions, and dreams for our communities and families into our giving. Gary suggests we think about both our immediate and our lifetime giving and estimate how much we want to contribute now and in the future.

Dorothy is a good example of someone who is following Gary's approach. She has always been generous with her time and money, but now that she's turned seventy, she's had a transformative shift in her thinking. "I'm deliberately looking for ways my money can have a real impact," she says. "As an example, I've gotten to know a recent immigrant and I've given him some money so his children can go to university. I recently said yes to a request from him for money so his wife could set up a stall in the market. I've decided that money means more to him than to me. So that's my consideration now—what the money means to somebody else versus what it means to me." Dorothy's thinking is also having an impact on her will. "I've changed my will to allocate 10 percent to philanthropic causes," she says, "and I've told my children. I also want to leave money for my nephews for their education."

"My attitude toward money has changed," she says, "and I'm not sure why. I think it doesn't mean so much to me now because I'm so happy with my life. I know I need to take care of my long-term needs, and they may be long indeed— my mother died when she was nearly one hundred. But I've decided I have enough money. So, my priorities have changed and I'm giving away more to worthy causes, and I'm giving money toward my grandchildren's education." Building a legacy of family memories is also part of Dorothy's thinking. "I'm spending money to travel with my children and grandchildren," she says, "and I've started taking my grandchildren on trips just by themselves. I took the whole family on a vacation this year. We piled in a van and went on a road trip. These are experiences that will burn bright in their memories."

My friend Eric is leaving a legacy by donating hours of volunteer time and expertise to an organization dedicated to alleviating the local housing crisis. Over decades of work with the non-profit, he has had the satisfaction of watching access to affordable housing transform the lives of many families. The organization has acknowledged his dedication by naming a building after him. Eric says he is honoured to have the recognition, but what pleases him more are the dozens of affordable homes now available in his community. The high-profile recognition that Eric has been given is an example of the ways that organizations are rewarding and acknowledging the importance of their volunteers. Increasingly, walls that list financial donors ranked by donation level now include volunteers listed by number of hours contributed.

I heard about a woman who has a dedicated approach to giving when I interviewed Nancy. Nancy spoke admiringly about a colleague who has formed a lifelong attachment to her chosen organization. "This woman has made a commitment to a particular organization dedicated to animal welfare," Nancy says. "I have been very impressed with the way she integrates her charitable giving into her life goals. She chooses to only work part-time because she doesn't want to spend any more of her day in the office. She has reduced her financial needs to meet that level of income, and her very tight budget always includes a contribution to her charity." Nancy learned this when she asked her colleague to make a Christmas donation to a worthy cause. The colleague explained that her charitable donation was already allocated. "Nothing would interfere with that commitment," Nancy says.

How Do I Choose My Legacy Cause?

Many of us aren't deeply committed to one cause, like my friend Eric's dedication to affordable housing or Nancy's friend's unwavering support for animal welfare. Even if we make regular charitable donations, we may do so without an overall strategy and are more likely to react to requests for help that randomly come our way. Maybe a friend is running a marathon for a worthy cause and asks for our support, or there's an annual campaign at work and our colleagues want to win the fundraising competition, or someone reaches out to us on social media and asks us to respond to an international crisis. A recent survey found that six in ten of us wait to be solicited by a charity before donating. It's the minority that is proactively pursuing information about a charitable cause.[5] That may change if we're thinking about our legacy.

John is someone who has always made a significant contribution to his community, and he now wants to leave a charitable bequest in his will. "I'm wondering whether I should make a big statement by leaving everything to one group," he says, "or leave smaller amounts to a larger number of organizations. I'm particularly interested in the area of children's mental health, and I want to contribute to an organization that measures its results. I'm looking for some place where I can achieve an outcome, rather than meet a need."

John says his big concern with leaving a bequest in his will is figuring out whether an organization will still be relevant in the future. "We know from research that an effective structure is very likely to result in an organization that will maintain its relevance moving forward," he says. "So, I need to look at an organization's governance structure. But, just to cover the bases, I should write a line in the will that will give the executor the flexibility to redirect my gift to a more appropriate choice if warranted."

If we're looking for an organization to support, Imagine Canada has developed a *Guide to Giving* with tips and information for making more meaningful contributions to the causes most important to us. As the guide explains, non-profit organizations are not all treated the same for tax purposes, and only a registered charity can issue a tax receipt. Some activist organizations cannot receive a charitable designation because of their political activities.[6] The CanadaHelps website has a section called "Personalized Discovery" to help you find charities and causes tailored to your interests.[7]

Tracy Gary's book, *Inspired Philanthropy* (discussed earlier), is a good tool if you want to leave a legacy and aren't sure where to begin, or if your giving strategy isn't working for you. The book includes worksheets and exercises to create a giving and legacy plan, provides questions to ask non-profits, and explains how to partner with advisers and non-profit leaders for outcomes. Gary's workbook exercises focus the mind, beginning as they do with our values and passions, and then asking us to be specific in identifying our mission, intention and desired outcomes.[8] The objective is to achieve more purposeful and satisfying personal giving. Her proposed tasks include discussing our plans with our family. Gary would like to see more transformative philanthropy that addresses the root causes of disadvantage, or promotes equitable living or sustains a healthy planet.

Peter Singer, author, philosopher and one of the founders of the effective altruism movement, says we need to maximize our impact on the planet by doing good in a cost-effective way. In his book *The Most Good You Can Do*, he gives examples of people who live modestly in order to give more. He cites Julia Wise as an example and includes a breakdown of her annual budget to explain how she can give surprisingly large amounts to charities despite living on a modest wage. He writes that even from a young age, Wise was aware that although she did not lack anything she needed, there were others who did. "Ever since, she has seen every dollar she spends as a dollar taken out of the hands of someone who needs it more than she does. So the question she asks herself is not how much she should give, but how much she should keep."[9]

Wise has a blog called *Giving Gladly*, where she discusses the charitable giving decisions that she and her husband make. They rely for advice on a website called *GiveWell*, which Singer says has taken the evaluation of charities to a new level. Singer writes, "If you give to one of GiveWell's top-rated charities, you can be confident that your donation will do good and be highly cost effective."[10] GiveWell's website currently recommends that donors give 70 percent of their annual donation to the Against Malaria Foundation and 30 percent to the Schistosomiasis Control Initiative.[11]

What Are Some Legacy Options?

There are a variety of charitable strategies that you can pursue while you're alive that will continue after your death. Over the decades, Claire has been an exceptional volunteer, donating countless hours to many worthy causes. When she turned sixty, people from all corners of her world came out in droves to celebrate her. For a birthday present, they collected money to establish a university scholarship fund in Claire's name in a field of study dear to her heart. But the scholarship was established well over a decade ago and Claire is not satisfied with its impact. "I'm so irritated about the scholarship fund," she says, "that I spoke to the university recently to complain. My fund has a big whack of money, but they only give a few thousand dollars each year to a couple of recipients. I never get a financial statement. I asked the donor relations person to give me a report. I want to know why they are giving out so little money, and I want to know how much publicity the university is giving to the availability of this scholarship." Claire is looking forward to getting the report she requested and is happy she's still alive and able to have this discussion with the university.

One of our challenges as donors is finding the right charitable fit that meets our expectations. Some version of the issue that Claire raises will be found with many endowed funds, which have a goal of preserving the capital of the fund and disbursing only the income. The author Malcolm Gladwell argues that universities would have more impact if they didn't hold such large endowments and instead set themselves higher spending goals. "The very fact that you set up an endowment means that you have decided before you start to minimize your impact," he says. "I'm going to take your dollar, and I'm going to commit to spending five cents of it every year. That's the craziest thing I've ever heard . . . If you have $40 billion and you're Harvard, how many interesting educational things could you do with $40 billion if you gave yourself a ten-year time horizon [to spend it all]?"[12] Claire has an advantage in this debate because she is still around to fight for her legacy. And if she's not happy with the results of her battle, she can make that known and reconsider any future commitments.

Another popular strategy for legacy giving is establishing a fund through a community foundation, which focuses on supporting local initiatives. Community foundations have been around for nearly a century and there are currently 191 of them across Canada, networked through the national Community Foundations of Canada. More than 90 percent of Canadian communities have access to a foundation, and you can find your nearest one through the national website.[13] Donations to the foundations come in all sizes and, depending on the community, relatively small amounts can allow you to establish your own fund. For example, in one community foundation, the current limit to set up your own fund is five thousand dollars, and this amount can be donated over ten years. So, if we were able to set aside ten dollars per week for ten years, we could make this happen. One of the benefits of establishing the fund now is that you can see the benefits while you're alive, and they will continue after your death.

An adviser on charitable giving says that if you intend to use a community foundation for your estate, there are advantages to setting up a fund while you're alive. "The fund forms a separate agreement that doesn't have to go into the will," she says. "The advantage of starting now is you can see how it works. The staff can advise you on setting up the parameters. You get the enjoyment of deciding on your priorities and naming the fund." However, there are limits to your control over your money. "Sometimes, people want themselves or their children to have full control over the assets," the adviser says, "but in a community foundation, you are only involved in an advisory capacity. You need to be aware that this is a transfer of assets and you have to relinquish the decision-making power. You are turning your money over to the foundation, so you have to trust them over the long run."

The adviser stresses the value of working with your community foundation while you're alive in order to get the best fit for your expectations. As well, she urges us to savour the enjoyment of making a contribution. "I don't think anyone should save all their giving for after their lifetime," she says. "There is such a lot of joy in the process."

Evan is glad he set up a family fund with the community foundation in the small town where his children were born, but he has some concerns. "Our family fund has given grants to several organizations over the years," he says, "often to sporting groups, maintaining cross-country ski trails, and other things that matter to our family. But I have been disappointed with some of the causes they have funded that are not our priorities." Also, Evan is not pleased that the foundation has increased its administrative costs. "They're arguing that if they have more operating revenue, they can raise more money," he says. "I've raised my concerns with the foundation staff. The problem is that most of the other donors are dead, so I need to be their voice as well." Despite his concerns, Evan is happy that his children will continue to be involved with the family fund, even after he's no longer alive. "They were born here and grew up here," he says, "and wherever life takes them, this fund will always keep them connected with their first home. As for me, I'm looking around for some new opportunities to donate more directly to something I really care about. I'm in the process of figuring that out and enjoying the process."

I asked an adviser on charitable giving about the issue of administrative costs that Evan raises. She says that charities and non-profits should be able to tell you what percentage of their budget they spend on different categories, including operations, fundraising and marketing, versus the amount that is allocated or disbursed to meet their goals. "These are important measures," she says. "But what you really need to know is the impact the organization is having, and that is much harder to measure. Sometimes, organizations have to spend more in the short term to meet their long-term objectives. As a donor, what you need to ask is, 'What are the results from my investment?'"

Another organization that plays a major role in many communities is the United Way, a federated network of over ninety local United Way offices in Canada. They are the largest non-governmental funder of social services locally and world-wide, and many of us have contributed to this impressive organization, often as part of their annual workplace drive. United Way doesn't run its own programs; rather, the organization raises money for social service programs offered by other charities, many of which are unable to do their own fundraising. United Way also researches community needs annually and allocates funds accordingly.

As someone who does not want to see their charitable donation being spent on donor recognition, I have been impressed with the United Way in this regard. When I was getting to know my local United Way office, I was invited to attend a donor luncheon, and I went principally to see how much donor money would be spent on the event. My concerns were alleviated when I found that our simple meal had been catered by one of the United Way recipient organizations, the bouquets of dandelions and daisies on the guest tables were in recycled bottles, and the speaker's talk was an in-depth analysis of the social issues facing the community and how the organization was responding. Subsequently, I was able to visit some of the organizations funded by United Way and provide some modest help by serving meals or handing out supplies. Such strategies go a long way toward persuading donors like me that my small contribution is well-placed.

The website of Charity Intelligence Canada provides some analytical tools to help us assess our giving decisions. Their searchable database has profiles on over seven hundred Canadian charities, and they assess each one on several measures: transparency and accountability, need for funding and cost efficiency.[14] However, they emphasize that the profiles don't provide information concerning the effectiveness of the charity's programs. If you're in discussion with these organizations, knowing their ratings can help you decide what questions to ask.[15]

All the experiences we have with charitable giving while we're alive will help us with our estate planning. If we decide to leave a bequest in our will, advisers recommend talking with the designated organization in advance of finalizing our plans so the group can better understand our goals, and we can educate ourselves about their mission. In *The 50 Biggest Estate Planning Mistakes . . . and How to Avoid Them*, Jean Blacklock and Sarah Kruger tell the story of a lawyer who avoided a costly error by having this conversation.

Her client wanted to leave a gift to a charity that operated a transportation service for seniors and people with disabilities, and she wanted the gift to cover the purchase of a van, as well as ongoing maintenance and repairs. However, as the lawyer found out, the charity could absolutely not accept gifts for repairs and upkeep because that was the responsibility of the municipal government. "Simply writing the client's original idea into the will would have resulted, at her death, in her executor spending extra time and professional fees to sort out the appropriate approach, with possibly a court application being required."[16]

There are many assets other than cash that can be used to provide a legacy benefit to an organization, including life insurance, securities, property and mutual funds, and we need to discuss the specifics of our case with our financial adviser and the charities involved. The CanadaHelps website provides information about the benefits of donating securities or mutual fund shares with an example of how it works.[17] In addition, many charitable organizations have someone on staff to help you think through your options.

However, just because you have something to give, don't assume you'll find a happy recipient. An adviser in charitable giving reminded me that organizations are not always set up to accept your non-monetary donations. "Some people want to donate material goods, such as houses, paintings or furniture, either for the organization to use or for resale. While this is a thoughtful gesture, organizations can be understaffed and ill-equipped to execute the donor's wishes." Other charities have well-designed programs to accept all matter of items and are set up to provide tax receipts and handle other aspects of your bequest. So, if you have goods to donate, look around for programs designed to handle these donations.

Among the many issues you need to consider regarding your bequest is whether you are looking for recognition, and in what form. I asked John about his feelings on this. He's the man I introduced you to earlier in this chapter who's trying to identify an organization for his bequest. John says he's of two minds regarding the issue of recognition. "I have absorbed my religion's messages about being modest," he says. "So, I would feel awkward about being publicized. But I also believe that living in a philanthropic way is an example of good behaviour that I want others to copy. It's good to serve as an example. I need to give this issue more thought."

Canadian charities and non-profits spend a lot of time trying to figure out whether donors want recognition and, if so, in what form. They think about this on a strategic basis, trying to find ways to marry forms of donor recognition with their organization's mission. When it comes to the individual donor, they are careful to be guided by personal preference on a case-by-case basis. One charitable adviser told me about helping a couple make a large gift to their church. The couple insisted the gift be anonymous. They had come into some money and didn't want other people in their congregation to know just how large a sum they had received. They were worried that information about their new-found wealth would change the way people viewed them. The adviser made the anonymous donation successfully and the couple's secret is safe.

As discussed earlier, one of the important trends in recognition is remembering the volunteers, not just the donors. One example is the donor wall associated with the Aanischaaukamikw Cree Cultural Institute in Oujé-Bougoumou, Quebec. The institute is designed to preserve and study the Cree culture and language, and the donor wall recognizes everyone who made the institute possible—both the donors who made financial contributions and the Cree elders who worked tirelessly to make it a reality. The institute's executive director says the donor wall is meaningful for the way "it ties our donors to the Cree Elders who promoted its development over the years."[18]

Developing a Family Legacy of Giving

One way to multiply the impact of your legacy is to nurture a family tradition of giving back. A recent national survey of parents found that 89 percent believe in inspiring their children to give to charities. When donors are asked what has inspired their charitable commitment, they often credit their upbringing and family modelling.[19] An important focus of the *Guide to Giving* on the Imagine Canada website is advice on how to create a family legacy of giving.[20]

In my book *Teens Gone Wired*, I describe the donation strategy our family established around Thanksgiving when our daughters were very young. We explained to them that at this time of year, we give thanks for our good fortune by choosing charities to support. When the practice started, they had no money of their own, so we allocated an amount for them to give to worthy causes of their choice. We'd review as a family the dozens of requests for support we'd received throughout the year. The children could decide to allocate their full amount to one organization or parcel it out to a number of groups. As their priorities changed over the years, so did their choices. Their decisions provided a window into their minds, and I really valued the insight into their preoccupations that I gained from the discussions. Now they have their own families and the legacy of giving continues.

Marion explains that she and her husband used a similar process to ours with their three children. They are young adults now and the impact of their annual giving program is plain to see. "The eldest always gave to wilderness protection," Marion says, "and I think she'll have a career working for the environment. The middle child was interested in food banks, and she just travelled to a developing country on a learning journey about food systems. She connected with the staff there and this has become her cause and maybe her career. The youngest always chose the local street mission. He believes in supporting the people who work in the second-hand store because they are being trained and supported by the community."

Marion values this approach to charitable giving because it has taught her children how society works and the importance of playing their part. "What is really important is understanding the value of non-profit organizations and their role in civil society," Marion says. "I think we have a scarcity mentality. That's why people don't give. They think they need to hang on to every cent because they'll never have enough. What people don't realize is you get back what you give. When I think about my own legacy, I realize the values we have instilled in our family will keep on giving long after I'm gone."

When Tracy Gary, the author of *Inspired Philanthropy*, was young, her grandmother made her a deal. "For every hour I volunteered and for every dollar I gave of my own money," she writes, "my grandmother would contribute a dollar to my 'giving fund' for future use."[21] Those of us with activist grandchildren and more limited means could quickly bankrupt ourselves, but some version of Gary's incentive strategy is worth considering. In Gary's case, her grandmother's program gave her the philanthropic bug, and Gramma's gift just keeps on giving.

Children vs. Charity

One of the challenges confronting people with children is how much to designate to charities in their wills. This is how Floyd describes his conundrum: "What is the right allocation between kids and charity on the death of the last parent? Early in life, my perspective was that I would give my kids a debt-free education and their first car, and after that, they were on their own. Everything else would go to charity. Then high housing costs came into the equation, so I want to help out there, both before and after death. But how much more should I give them? If you are part of the Gates-Buffett pledge, you leave 'a majority' to charity. But in the case of the wealthy, that still leaves a massive residual for the children. What about the rest of us? This is a complex issue that depends in part on the kids' needs and expectations, and I'm wondering how to strike the right balance."

Floyd is referring to the Giving Pledge, which was founded in 2010 by Warren Buffett and Bill and Melinda Gates to encourage wealthy people to contribute the majority of their wealth to philanthropic causes. The action was inspired by "the example set by millions of people at all income levels who give generously—and often at great personal sacrifice—to make the world better."[22] About thirty years ago, billionaire investor Warren Buffett was quoted as saying he wanted to leave his kids "enough money so that they would feel they could do anything, but not so much that they could do nothing." After putting his two sons and a daughter through college, he planned to give most of his money to his charitable foundation. He believed that providing his heirs with "a lifetime supply of food stamps just because they came out of the right womb" was both harmful for them and an anti-social act.[23]

Former New York City mayor Michael Bloomberg is one of the 175 billionaires from twenty-two countries who have signed the Giving Pledge. He says he plans to invest in philanthropic organizations rather than bequeathing his millions directly to his daughters. "If you want to do something for your children and show how much you love them," he writes in his pledge, "the single best thing—by far—is to support organizations that will create a better world for them and their children. And by giving, we inspire others to give of themselves, whether their money or their time."[24]

Floyd is far from alone in worrying about the financial needs of his adult children. In a recent poll, over three-quarters of parents with children over the age of eighteen said they would give their children financial support to help them move out, get married or move in with a partner. High-priced housing and the tough job market for young adults are factors in their thinking. Giving money to your adult children while you are alive rather than waiting until after you're gone lets you watch them enjoy the money and, also, avoids probate fees (estate administration taxes).[25] One of the expressions used for this approach is "giving with warm hands."

When I asked an estate lawyer whether her clients who have children are leaving money in their wills to charity, she answered that it depends on the size of the estate and the age of the children. "If there's enough money, then the answer is yes," she says. "They feel there's enough money to both satisfy their children's needs and leave a bequest to their favourite charities. For smaller estates, it depends on the age of the children. By the time my older clients are revising their wills, their children might be in their fifties and more financially secure. At that point, they feel they can place greater emphasis on charitable donations."

One approach is to treat charity as a child. So, if you have three children, you divide your estate four ways and leave a quarter to charity. That being said, Katy Basi, a Toronto estate lawyer, recommends leaving a precise dollar amount to charity rather than a percentage of the value of your estate. This allows for more effective tax planning and means that the charity doesn't have to be involved in the administration of the estate to ensure they get every penny owed.

Regardless of how you want to handle your charitable donation, Basi says you need to tell your children up front. "There are many cases where people are reliant on an inheritance, rack up debt and then learn after their parents die that much of the money they counted on is actually going to charity," she says. "Parents aren't doing their kids any favours by not talking to them about their plans for their estate."[26] I would add that you shouldn't wait until your will is written before talking with your children. Consult with them in advance. You may find them much more supportive of your thinking about the value of generosity than you imagine, and they may have some good ideas of their own to contribute to your thinking. Perhaps you'll be able to create a family legacy of giving that will continue contributing through the generations.

Social Ventures

When your expertise lies in business management, taking those skills into the non-profit sector might be the best way of giving back. This was the case for Wayne. He spent decades working for large corporations and serving as a volunteer on non-profit boards. Then he decided he could be more effective by moving into a smaller, more entrepreneurial approach—in both his for-profit and non-profit activities. "Initially, I was on boards of long-established traditional charities," he says, "where the prime responsibility of board members tends to be leading fundraising initiatives in support of the organization—arts, culture, health care, education, et cetera. Then I shifted into venture capital—funding and helping start-ups, first investing other peoples' money and then, as an 'angel,' investing my own funds. So, I started to apply these same principles of innovation to the philanthropic sector through social venture partnerships. My philanthropic activities came to mirror my venture investing activities."

Wayne cites SVP Vancouver as an example of "social venture partnership." The organization currently has 155 partners who are entrepreneurs and business leaders providing selected non-profit organizations with both capital and expertise. Established in 2001, the organization has contributed more than six million dollars and thousands of volunteer hours to more than fifty-seven non-profits in their community. "Social venture is about bringing venture capital principles to non-profits and applying innovative, entrepreneurial models around education, employment of people with barriers, helping youth at risk, homeless, et cetera," Wayne says.

The SVP Vancouver website gives examples of the non-profits they support and those that have "graduated." Current recipients include Take a Hike, which offers a full-time alternative education program engaging at-risk youth through adventure-based learning, academics, therapy and community involvement; Learning Disabilities Association Vancouver, which wants to empower every child and youth in Greater Vancouver with a learning disability to achieve lifelong success and happiness; and PEDAL Society, a bike shop and social enterprise that supports youth by offering mechanical repair training, access to bicycles and the skills to ride safely. SVP has chapters in over forty cities around the world.[27]

Over the past five years, Wayne's for-profit investing activities have also narrowed into only cause-related businesses. "Many not-for-profits have no way to become sustainable through revenues and must be funded philanthropically," he says. "But others are in good cause-related businesses; for example, employing people with barriers. There are opportunities to grow those entities via for-profit investment capital like loans." As an example, Wayne cites CleanStart, a Vancouver-based company offering junk removal, hoarding cleanup and pest control. The vision of company founder Dylan Goggs is to reduce waste and create as many jobs as possible for people with barriers to employment.[28] To pursue these kinds of investment opportunities, Wayne participates in Toniic, "the global action community for impact investors." "Whereas SVP is purely philanthropic," Wayne explains, "Toniic acts as an investment club for investors in mission-based businesses who expect a financial return rather than a tax credit for donations."[29]

Wayne's goal is to form a personal foundation that will donate to charities like SVP and the creative organizations it supports. The foundation's capital would be invested in mission-based organizations that generate a reasonable investment income. "I want something that our kids can continue to manage after my wife and I are gone," he says. Wayne is getting closer to his goal thanks to funds he will receive from the buyout of one of his tech investments. He is doing his homework on the best vehicle for his foundation and is leaning toward CHIMP. CHIMP describes itself as giving everyone their own free foundation, along with a toolset that allows them to give to and fundraise for any registered charity in Canada, on their own or with friends, family and social networks.[30] Wayne likes the simplicity of CHIMP's high-tech platform and its service levels and flexibility.[31]

Wayne's example may seem far removed from the world of charitable giving that many of us inhabit, but his story contains lessons that are broadly applicable. When we're thinking about donating money to an organization, we should also consider whether contributing our skills and expertise could make a difference. And if we come into some financial means through hard work, inheritance or luck of the draw, we should consider how to turn that money into a vehicle that keeps on giving.

"In Memoriam" Donations

When someone dies, the obituary will often identify an organization where people can make an in memoriam donation in the name of the deceased loved one. As I wrote earlier, since KS's death, I've started asking people what group they would choose to receive donations in their memory. This question requires people to identify an organization or a cause they would most like to be associated with at the time of their death. Not everyone has an immediate answer. Although lots of us donate time and money to a variety of organizations, it's a tough call to decide which one would best represent our time here on earth and our hopes for the future.

When I asked Meredith if she could identify an organization she would like people to donate to in her memory, she admitted to being at a loss. "I have no idea," she said. "I'm going to set myself the goal of figuring this out. I'd want to designate a group I'd been directly involved with. And I'd want a history with the organization, say a ten-year commitment of volunteering. I haven't found a group I could do this with yet, but I'm looking." Nancy also couldn't name an in memoriam recipient when I interviewed her. She has recently changed jobs and feels her decision is going to be easier. "I work for an organization reporting on the environment," she says. "So, I get a close look at lots of different groups and can see their level of effectiveness first-hand. I'm starting to narrow the field."

When I told a financial adviser that I was asking people to identify an in memoriam recipient, she thought it was a good idea. "If you don't discuss this issue in advance with your loved ones," she said, "they are left to make their own decisions on your behalf. Unfortunately, what I've seen happen too many times is that people focus on the way someone died, rather than on the way they lived. When people ask for my advice about memorial donations, I always start with the question, 'What were your loved one's interests?' But in the moment of grief, people don't always think that way, and they end up memorializing people by the circumstances of their death. But this shouldn't define their lives. To avoid this, try and have these conversations while you're alive."

This is a good point at which to revisit my misgivings about the legacy of KS. As I wrote earlier, I felt that the choice of a lecture series at the local university for her in memoriam donations was limited, touching, as it did, on only one aspect of her complex and multi-faceted impact on her world. But I had no way of knowing how KS would have wanted to be remembered, and I regretted never asking her. So, I decided to give my assumptions some deeper scrutiny. After reaching out to KS's colleagues, friends and family to ask their opinions, I concluded that my concern was misplaced.

KS's son told me he was grateful for the lecture series. He has attended a number of the lectures, and they solidified his knowledge of his mother's professional contribution and added to his understanding of her impact on the lives of others. "As well, I learned that she brought the same warmth and sense of humour into her work that I experienced at home," he says. "And I saw how she touched others with her joy."

When I asked KS's sister for her opinion, she was confident that KS would have been happy with leaving the university connection as her legacy. "She really enjoyed teaching there," she says. "Her legacy is about being a woman breaking into her field, which was really difficult at the time. She was in the forefront and it's nice to have this acknowledged. And our mother was still alive when KS died, and this tribute made her very proud."

KS's colleague told me that along with the lecture series, there is a scholarship awarded every year in KS's honour. The recipient will often write a thank-you note to KS's family, referring to what KS's accomplishments have meant to them. As well, I learned that the lecture series was not the only in-memoriam tribute. In the obituary placed in the local paper, the family requested donations to the neighbourhood food bank. The donors received a thank-you note from the family, saying that KS "always and everywhere cared for people." In addition, there are two benches with commemorative plaques for KS in neighbourhood parks. The plaques acknowledge that she "actively contributed a great deal of caring, time and energy to her friends and community." So I can see that more sides of my dear KS have found the light of day in her legacy.

In addition to a legacy of tributes after her death, while she was alive, KS left a recording of herself for her family. The next chapter looks at the many ways we leave pieces of ourselves that live on after we've gone.

Leaving a Piece of Ourselves

People say that leaving behind their values and life lessons to their family is more important to their legacy than passing on financial assets.[1] "Pass on your values, not just your valuables" is the credo. On a daily basis, we convey our messages about right thinking and right acting through our thoughts and deeds. In addition, some people want to pass along their values in a more structured way. One form this may take is an "ethical will." Unlike a legal will, the ethical will is not concerned with distributing our material assets. Its purpose is to pass values from one generation to the next by sharing life stories, lessons learned, dreams for the future and expressions of love, forgiveness and hope.

Sydney introduced me to the concept of an ethical will. "The philosophy behind ethical wills is sharing what your life has meant to you and how you want the next generation to live," he says. "You're telling your family what you want them to take forward from your life, into their lives. Recently, my niece was left an ethical will by her father. He had bound his document in five volumes, with a copy for each of his children."

Sydney recommends the book *Hebrew Ethical Wills*, which has been a source of inspiration for many people when composing their own legacy document. First published in 1926, the two-volume book, edited by Israel Abrahams, is a compilation of ethical wills written by prominent people.

Daniel Gottlieb published what serves as an ethical will in his book *Letters to Sam: A Grandfather's Lessons on Love, Loss, and the Gifts of Life*. When Sam was born, Gottlieb had been a quadriplegic for twenty years as the result of a car accident. His letters to Sam share his experience as a practising psychologist, combined with the insights he gained from his disability. "Books taught me a bit about psychology," he wrote. "But paralysis taught me to sit still and keep my ears and heart open so I could listen."[2]

Gottlieb started out writing the letters after Sam's birth to tell him about life and help him get to know his grandfather. Then, at fourteen months, Sam was diagnosed with a severe form of autism. "Now I also wanted him to understand what it means to be 'different' from everybody else," Gottlieb wrote. "I wanted to teach him what I've learned about fighting against the kind of adversity that I face almost daily and that I fear he will face in his life. And I wanted to tell him how peace comes to us when we simply stop fighting." But most of all, Gottlieb wanted to tell his grandson about love.[3]

If we know our life is ending, the motivation to pass along our values to the next generation can loom large. Dr. Harvey Max Chochinov, a professor of psychiatry at the University of Manitoba, has developed a program he calls Dignity Therapy, which helps terminally ill patients record their stories and life lessons. Therapists audiotape patients talking about what matters most to them, and the transcripts provide a record for family and friends. Family members have found the process valuable, both for the dying person and for the grieving family. Here is an example of family feedback: "I think the Dignity Therapy truly helped him [the terminally ill patient] feel as though he were doing something useful and to be able to leave behind a part of himself. That in turn has helped myself and the children as it is almost like receiving a special gift of his words that we can have for our lifetime."[4]

But we don't need to wait for a terminal illness to start recording our life lessons. Nor should we put the process off to some future point in time that may never come. One year, as a birthday present, my daughters compiled a remarkable scrapbook for me. They asked friends I'd known for decades to write me a letter about what our friendship meant to them, and to include stories and photos. My daughters also included their own letters of thanks to me. The result is an in-depth look at love, community and adventure. I laughingly call this "my long-term-care" book. If I lose my memories, I'll revisit this book to enjoy afresh the stories of great friends and fun times. And if I'm being cared for by strangers, these tales will help them know who I am. In an unstructured way, this document serves as my ethical will, conveying my life lessons for future generations as perceived through the eyes of my family and friends.

Letters from the Grave

Sometimes, people put their final thoughts in letters intended to be found after their death. They may leave the letter with their will, as was the case with my friend KS, which you read about earlier. As soon as one of KS's colleagues learned about her death, she went in search of the letter and delivered it to her sons. Within hours of losing their mother, they were able to read, in her own handwriting, about her love for them and why she had made the decisions she did about her estate.

Other people may leave a personal note amidst their belongings, to be found when their possessions are being dispersed. This was the case for one family that was gathered at their dying mother's bedside when they found a small envelope addressed to her children. The note was buried in the bottom layer of their mother's jewellery box, and the children found it while going through the few things that remained of their mother's after years spent in a long-term care facility. The note had been written twenty years earlier, well before she developed dementia. It read: "To my beloved children: I love you all deeply and am proud of you all. You all have succeeded at your particular callings and have good spouses who are loving and supportive of you. I am happy about that. Have long, healthy lives and have fun! Mom. P.S. Great grand-kids, too."

When I asked the children how they felt about the note, some of the reactions may not have been what their mother hoped for. One son felt that his mother "was trying to convince herself of something." Another said he would not be leaving a similar note for his children. "I gave my children the ability to create their own independent, successful lives without needing to look to me for approval," he says. "I suppose my message to my children would be similar to my mother's note, but the approach is very different since it goes unsaid." All the children were in agreement that the note said a lot about their mother and her love for them. "It shows how much she cared about us. Along with her love, she thought we needed and wanted her approval. And just in case that was in any doubt, she gave us that as her legacy."

If there are no letters or final communications, we need to hope the positive qualities of the relationship will speak for themselves. My daughter found she could fall back on this certainty when her grandfather died and she knew that their love for one another was never in doubt. "I couldn't be at Grandpa's bedside when he died and it broke my heart," she recalled. "I thought I needed to be there to tell him I loved him one last time. But then you reminded me, Mom, that there was nothing left unsaid between Grandpa and me. We both knew we loved each other deeply. Thinking about that really helped me in my grief."

Sometimes in situations where a message from the deceased could have made amends or served to heal some wounds, people take their silence to the grave. This was the case for Gloria's friend. "My friend always had a difficult relationship with her mother," Gloria says, "but she wanted to do the right thing. So, when her mother got too ill to take care of herself, my friend moved her closer and took care of her until her death. The mother never thanked her daughter and, indeed, never showed the slightest sign that she loved her or appreciated what she was doing for her. She died without a kind or loving word for her daughter crossing her lips."

After the death, Gloria went with her friend to help her clean out her mother's room. "My friend was hoping desperately to find a will," Gloria says, "and I found an envelope that looked like it might be what she was looking for. I gave her the document and left her alone to read the paper in private. When I returned, she was sobbing. It was indeed the will, written in a form that was dry as dust, and there was no personal letter. That woman left no shred of expression of love or caring for her child. And now it was over. I thought it was utterly heartless of the mother not to reach out in some way, even from the grave."

Standing in stark contrast is the story of Lisa Lawson, who wants to make sure that her son never doubts her love for him. When Lawson's story appeared in the *Toronto Star*, she had been living with breast cancer for seven years. She found the most difficult aspect of her prognosis was thinking about her son's future. "He's such a happy little boy and he's going to be a different person because I won't be there . . . " she says. "I really want Luke to have positive memories of me and the kind of person I am." Luke was eight years old at the time of the interview, and Lawson had bought birthday cards for him for every year until he turns twenty-one. She also has cards to celebrate what she imagines will be his future events—his university graduation, wedding, first home and first baby. She plans to leave behind scrapbooks and videos, as well as gifts for her parents and her sister.[5]

If we're determined to communicate from the grave, there are digital services to consider. Currently, such services start up and fade away or get reinvented, so picking an organization today that will still be around when it's needed can be a challenge. At the time of writing, a product called SecretValet will store information for delivery to a third party after your death. The person does not need to know the information is waiting for them. A YouTube video produced by SecretValet shows a tear-inducing scenario in which a teenager celebrating his eighteenth birthday is surprised by the appearance on his desktop of a pre-recorded video from his deceased parents, sending him their birthday wishes.[6]

Another service, an iPhone app called Incubate:The Digital Time Capsule, lets you send messages to any mobile number in the United States, whether it be text, photos or videos, and schedule an exact time for transmission up to twenty-five years into the future. Incubate's creator launched his online site by recording a message from his grandmother sending Thanksgiving holiday wishes. After her death, a half-dozen people received her message.[7] These services raise countless questions: "What if this current technology has been overtaken by unrecognizable developments?" "What if a computer glitch sends out your announcement prematurely?" "What if people change their email addresses or phone numbers?" But it's fun to ponder the possibilities.

The big risk we take in sending messages into the future is that our words will arrive in a different world. The hopes we had for our children when we wrote our missives may not be the hopes they have for themselves when they eventually read our thoughts. Our wishes for their happiness could imply specific goals for them in their career, relationships or family, rather than liberate them to find their own path. Hopefully, our legacy will include sufficient love that the readers of our notes or digital messages will interpret them with compassion and realize that we had the best of intentions.

Sometimes, of course, we don't have the best of intentions. For example, there was the case you read about earlier where the man wrote in his will that his daughter was to use his one-thousand-dollar bequest to throw a party and dance on his grave. But even here, although the message may have seemed clear to the father, did the daughter read it the right way?

Candy Schulman wrote in the *New York Times* about being grateful her mother had reached out to her with a message from the grave. Schulman had felt neglected by her mother when she was growing up and regretted never hearing from her any words of praise. The first time they cradled each other, Schulman's mother was ninety years old and had just confessed that she had grown up in an orphanage. Schulman was fifty-three at the time and was relieved to finally learn the details of her mother's past. About six years after that conversation, her mother died. When Schulman was cleaning out her mother's apartment, she found an envelope labelled "to be opened only after my death." In the envelope was an audiotape her mother had recorded that began with the words, "I grew up in an orphanage." "I made copies of the tape to distribute to her eight grandchildren," Schulman wrote, "grateful that they could finally hear her story in her own words. Just as Mom had chosen how to die, she had determined how to share her legacy."[8]

Transferring Skills

Another way our legacy is shared is through the skills we transfer to our loved ones. When Terry was told she was dying of brain cancer, she decided that one of her legacies would be making sure her sons could cook a turkey dinner. "People talk about how brave I am," she said, "but they don't know how sad I am. I think of my family without a woman and I feel I'm deserting them. So here is my legacy: I'm sending my boys out into the world knowing how to make a Christmas dinner." After Terry's diagnosis, various treatments gave her two more years of life. With that precious gift of time, she was able to assist her boys in preparing a couple of Christmas and Thanksgiving meals, and to watch them become more competent and confident cooks. "The boys carried off Christmas beautifully," she told me after her final Christmas. "They found out that it's not that easy to get six different components all hot and to the table at the same time. But they pulled it off splendidly." I can't imagine those boys ever cooking a turkey dinner without thinking of their beloved mother and thanking her for her gift to them. And those special meals will always be more flavourful having been steeped in her love.

Recipes are favourite components of legacies because food and drink are imbued with such powerful memories. Some people bind their recipes in book form and gift them to children or grandchildren. My aunt had a groundbreaking career with a multinational company promoting the use of spices in cooking—this during an era when practically the only zest in Canadian cuisine was salt and pepper. She developed her own tasty recipes using her company's flavourings and demonstrated the food preparation in kitchens across the country. We have a collection of her favourite recipes, and eating a piece of her onion cheese bread, toasted and spread with melting butter, materializes her in our kitchen. At Christmas, it's my mother who is invoked by thoughts of her rich and delicious squares, which we helped her package into gift tins, sampling mightily in the process. Food offers legacies of multi-dimensional remembrances of tastes, smells, celebration and love.

When it comes to skills transfer, my father's legacy burns bright every time his children, his grandchildren and their partners are on a ski hill. Dad was a passionate skier, having started at a young age in Montreal as a member of his high school and then his university ski-touring clubs. His skiing lore included wild tales of building the first lifts at Mont Tremblant, and military manoeuvres on skis in the Italian Alps as part of his World War II service. Dad was determined to pass his passion along to his children—against great odds. Circumstances were far from favourable for his dream because for most of our formative years, we lived in a city in a flat part of the country. The local ski hill, which we called "the pimple," was the edge of a small ravine, and standing in the ski lift line took longer than doing the downhill run.

On snowy winter weekends when we weren't at the local ski club, you'd find us on a hair-raising drive about two and a half hours north to a real ski hill. Dad would get us up in the freezing cold, pitch-black early morning and load our gear into the car. We'd ski all day, and then we'd make the drive home that same night. My brothers and I can get into hysterics reminding one another of the terrors of driving in the dark through intense snowstorms—conditions that made the worst ski runs look tame.

When Dad became a grandfather, he transferred his commitment to turning out decent skiers to his grandchildren. All in all, my father was remarkably successful. Most of our family members genuinely enjoy skiing, and several have earned good money over the years as ski instructors and coaches. On a blue-sky day, carving down a sparkling slope with snow rooster-tailing off the back of my skis, I often think of my father. Without him, I'm not sure I'd be there.

Things with Heart and Soul

And then there's the legacy of our possessions. We're urged to clean up our stuff so it's not a burden to those we leave behind, but we should avoid sweeping the slate too clean. When I ask people about their family's legacy, small personal items figure large, especially if they are perceived as embodying life lessons and family values. Examples abound: clothing people inherited that they wear fondly because it is soaked in memories of the previous owner, art that has a known and treasured provenance, handmade items that carry the stories of generations, and heritage jewellery refashioned as contemporary symbols of love and commitment. Things become part of our legacy if we imbue them with ourselves.

Jennifer's mother had a lifetime hobby of quilt-making, and for Jennifer, the interconnected pieces of fabric contain their shared history. "In many of her quilts, I can recognize clothing we used to wear," she says. "The women in Mom's quilting group called themselves 'The Gaggle,' and when I look at her lovely handiwork, I can hear their laughter, and I can feel their kindness. They supported Mom though Dad's death and through the pain of Mom's failing eyesight. It may look like a quilt to someone else, but to me, it's a lifetime of caring and community. After Mom died, we gave one of her quilts to each of her grandchildren. Every time they wrap themselves in this work made with their grandmother's hands, they feel the love she gave and the love she received."

When my mother asked us to choose what we wanted of her things, I selected two small boxes that she had reworked using photos of her mother. Mom was a nurse by training and a volunteer by passion, and crafts were not her thing. But she had a short period of working with decoupage, and these were two of her pieces. The white marble box is topped with an exquisite photo of my grandmother, taken when she was in her late teens or early twenties. The photo shows her from the waist up, in an elaborate white lace dress with a gold necklace on her bare neck, romantically gazing down in half profile. Inside the box, my mother taped a note in her distinctive handwriting: "'Olive May' this belongs to Lyndsay Green." The other piece is a small wooden music box that plays "Love Story." The image that covers its top is a photo of my smiling grandmother holding my mother as a baby.

I never met my grandmother because she died when my mother was eighteen, and looking at these boxes can still make me cry for my mother's loss. There is never a good time to lose a mother, but the teenage years are particularly bad. I regret never having met this woman, but she looms large for me because of the stories about her that have been cemented in our family. We are told Olive May was warm and loving and had a great sense of humour. She was convent-taught and played the piano and had a beautiful alto voice. During the Depression, hungry men would knock on her kitchen door and they would always find a meal and a seat at her table. When I look at my treasured boxes, I channel her spirit and remember her values.

My friend KS left behind a unique piece of herself. About a decade before she was killed, she recorded a CD of herself singing lullabies. The songs were ones her mother had sung to her at bedtime, and she, in turn, had sung them to her children. When KS told me that she was going to make the recording, she explained that her sons had urged her to do this. And she also recognized what a lovely gift it would make for her mother to have her bedtime songs memorialized in this way. The recording would give her mother's grandchildren, and generations to come, access to her musical legacy. KS decided to work with a recording studio and produced a very professional-sounding recording of twenty-one songs in which her lovely voice is unaccompanied, as though she were singing her little ones to sleep.

I asked KS's son what this recording of his mother singing her bedtime songs meant to him. He admitted he hadn't listened to the CD for more than a decade because it had been stored away when he was moving around. But he remembered how he felt when he first heard it. "To be honest, I recall being taken aback when I first heard it," he says, "since the produced sound felt a long way from the experience of lying in bed next to her while she sang. So, I weirdly never really listened to it much at the time, despite having agitated for some kind of recording. I think I was driven primarily by strong nostalgia for the experience of being sung to sleep. Ironically, I think that a low-quality recording on something like one of today's cellphones probably would have been more satisfying to me, originally. I remember some other relatives playing it for babies though, and I'm going to track down my copy and listen to it again."

I listened afresh to the CD and understand what KS's son means. The voice on the recording, lovely as it is, doesn't really sound like KS. She has been distanced from us by the professional recording process. While I was listening to the CD, a contrasting recording of KS's voice leapt unbidden to my mind. After KS's death, for what seemed like weeks, the family left her recorded voice message on the home answering machine. It was one of those standard messages saying she would return our call just as soon as possible. She was completely alive in that recording and it broke my heart. Every time I called the house, I would steel myself to prepare for hearing her voice, but I couldn't stop my emotional response. I would sob into the phone, knowing my words would be incomprehensible, but confident that someone would recognize it was me and return my call.

As with the CD, I feel a similar distance from a painting of KS that the family gave me. The portrait was commissioned by her boyfriend and painted from a photograph. It is a nice piece of art and the framed copy I received is of beautiful quality, but it could be of anyone. When I want to bring KS into the room, instead of looking at the portrait, I look at her snapshots, ones we took of our trips together and others she sent me over the years. A few years after her death, I gave her sons each a framed collage of photos of their mom taken during her teenage years. I knew they would welcome a more intimate portrait of their mother, and I was right; the gift brought tears to their eyes.

Sometimes, we bequeath our things in the hope they will be appreciated and the impact is beyond our expectation. This was the case when the artist Doris McCarthy left "her angel" to her long-time friend, a woman who was also executive of the

West Parry Sound Health Centre. The wooden angel had been carved and crafted into a weather vane in 1940 and was on the roof of McCarthy's home for over half a century. In 2014, the "Northern Angel" was established as the health centre's icon, and it is used in their foundation's fundraising campaign. McCarthy had been able to stay in her summer studio on Georgian Bay well into her advanced years thanks to the centre's expert care, so this celebration of her angel was a fitting memorial.[9]

These stories show the beauty in meaningful remembrances; however, there is a big difference between leaving a legacy of a few significant treasures and dumping a home full of stuff on our descendants. For my book *You Could Live a Long Time: Are You Ready?* I interviewed Norah, who had to clear out her parents' house after they both died at age seventy-three. She tackled the task on her own, and it took her a year and a half to complete. "I was close to my parents and felt duty-bound to do a careful job," she says. "I gave things to forty-three individuals and institutions, including the War Museum and the Anglican Archives. That's why it took me so long. And I was teaching at the same time." Now Norah is worrying about what to do with her own possessions. "Looking forward, my biggest issue is trying to give my things to people who will value them," she says. "I don't want to leave this job for others when I die."

The Swedes have a custom called "death cleaning," which means doing a deep clean of our possessions, and it can be done at any age. Margareta Magnusson wrote *The Gentle Art of Swedish Death Cleaning* to help free us and our families from a lifetime of clutter. Magnusson is "between eighty and one hundred years old." She writes, "I have death cleaned so many times for others, I'll be damned if someone has to death clean after me."[10] Her tips are very practical for helping us get rid of things that no longer have meaning. But the most lyrical part of her book is her admiration for a beautiful desk from the 1700s. "We sit and write at it, and always wonder what has been written on it. Who wrote sitting there hundreds of years ago? What were they writing? ...A love letter? A business deal? A confession?"[11] The desk belongs to a friend who will sell it soon, but not before writing a small note and tucking it inside. Magnusson hopes the tradition will continue and that everyone who writes on the desk will leave a record.

In the next section, we turn from leaving objects that are imbued with meaning for the recipients, to leaving actual parts of ourselves.

Actual Parts of Ourselves

In the above examples, people are leaving metaphorical pieces of themselves as part of their legacy. Another aspect of our legacy can be giving away actual parts of ourselves. We could, for example, donate our organs for transplant. The Canadian Transplant Society tells us that 90 percent of Canadians support organ and tissue donation, but less than 20 percent have made plans to donate. One donor can benefit more than seventy-five people and save up to eight lives.[12] And we can gift our body or specific parts of it to science. The Concussion Legacy

Foundation, for example, accepts pledges to donate our brain to their brain bank to support research on chronic traumatic encephalopathy (CTE). Opened in 2008, the brain bank focuses on concussions and other consequences of brain trauma. The foundation's research revealed the first cases of CTE in athletes whose primary exposure was soccer, rugby, baseball, ice hockey, college football and high school football.[13]

In 2016, Dylan Matthews, a co-founder and journalist at the US-based news site *Vox*, donated his left kidney to someone he'd never met and whose name he didn't know. Matthews was twenty-six years old. "The only thing I knew about him [the recipient] at the time was that he needed my kidney more than I did," Matthews wrote. "It would let him avoid the physically draining experience of dialysis and possibly live an extra nine to ten years, maybe more." Matthews's donation was a trade with a relative of the recipient who wasn't a match and resulted in a chain of donations that led to four people getting kidneys.

Matthews wants people to know that donating a kidney is not that hard to do, provided you have an understanding employer, paid medical leave and friends and family willing to support you in the recovery. He says he's wanted to give a kidney for years since he first heard it was possible, after reading about good Samaritan kidney donors when he was in college. "It just seemed like such a simple and clear way to help someone else, through a procedure that's very low risk to me," he wrote.

Matthews says that, in contrast to other decisions he's made in his life, he has no regrets about donating his kidney. He says that being an adult is hard and you're going to get a lot of choices wrong, "about your career, about your friendships, about your romantic life, about your family." But when it came to the kidney donation, he was "selfishly, deeply gratified to have made at least one choice in my life that I know beyond a shadow of a doubt was the right one."[14]

Two years after Matthews's procedure, German Lopez, another *Vox* employee, donated his kidney and credited Dylan Matthews as his inspiration. He tweeted about the experience and how gratifying it was that, as a result of his donation, a twenty-three-year-old woman received a life-saving kidney, and a chain of two or more people would also be receiving kidneys. In addition, Lopez came out of the process a healthier person. "One side bonus in this entire process was that the extensive tests for the past 10 months helped make me healthier. They uncovered a minor heart condition (WPW) and pushed me to get it cured," he tweeted. He provided a link for US readers who want to get the kidney donation process started and explained why he wanted to publicize his donation. "It feels strange talking about all of this in public (as if I'm trying to show off), but I want to communicate that this is something that really is possible to do," he wrote.[15]

Given the growing number of people who have tattoos, we're likely to see an interest in passing along this skin art as part of legacy planning.[16] Some services claim to be able to remove and save tattoos so they can be bequeathed like other property. In 2015, Charles Hamm, founder of a non-profit organization dedicated to this process, was interviewed on the CBC Radio show *q*. Hamm said he wanted the actual piece of art that was part of him, not merely a replica, to be preserved. "The people who will get this will know what they meant to me," he said. Hamm feels that his tattoos form an important part of his legacy. "My tattoos recognize certain aspects of my life," he said. "I have a lizard on my arm that my grandson drew, and monkeys that my daughter enjoys. I have a gorilla that is guarding my wife. My daughter said, 'I want the monkeys.' They have all claimed a piece of my skin art."[17]

Some people have eggs, fertilized embryos or sperm stored at fertility clinics and will need to consider the legal considerations of bequeathing this material or authorizing someone to make decisions about its use. And then there are the people who want to preserve their entire bodies, just in case the future will have ways of restoring them to life. If you want your body to be retained for this potential eventuality, you'll need to entrust it to someone who will invest the time and money to keep you at your best.

In 2016, a British High Court ruled in favour of a fourteen-year-old girl who was dying of cancer and wanted her body to be cryogenically frozen after her death. The court got involved after her parents disagreed over her request. The court ruling gave the girl's mother, who supported her daughter's wishes, the sole right over her daughter's body. The girl wrote to the court, "I think being cryo-preserved gives me a chance to be cured and woken up, even in hundreds of years' time. I don't want to be buried underground. I want to live and live longer and I think that in the future they might find a cure for my cancer and wake me up." The mother has now made a commitment for her lifetime and beyond. Her will should either provide financing to support her daughter's wishes or entrust her daughter's body to someone else who agrees to make a moral and financial commitment to freezing and preserving it. And that responsibility should be passed on down the line until, or if, the young girl is woken up, as she hopes.[18]

Conclusion

Our death does not end the development of our legacy. Even after our bodies have been put to rest, our character will keep moving on. Who we are in our universe and what the world thinks of us continue to be formed and revised, even when we're gone. I watched this happen when people talked to me about their departed family members and friends and imbued them with the emotional fibre of those who are still alive. As their stories were being told, the deceased leapt into our conversations, sometimes radiating kindness and consideration, other times trailing chains of hurt and anger.

If we take our legacy seriously, we'll put our lives under a microscope and assess whether our pursuits and our behaviour are consistent with our goals and our values. After this scrutiny, we might decide to refocus our lives to realize unfulfilled dreams while there is still time, or to follow new-found convictions. We might decide to give more to others through volunteering and charitable donations, including bequests we could set up while we're alive.

If we act with an eye to a future-without-us, we might find the courage to deal with the fallout from difficult decisions. We might face our responsibility to clean up our mess—not just those unsorted papers and piles of memorabilia—but the personal entanglements that, if left untended, can leave heartache and acrimony. We might be clear about our bequests and provide fulsome explanations, articulated with compassion and love. We might take steps to minimize the pain of those we leave behind. Maybe if our lives are driven by good values, we might even inspire others to continue our legacy.

The people I interviewed for this book were provoked by their musings about legacy, and many told me about their personal resolutions. One of KS's colleagues is going to write a letter to her family and leave it with her will—as KS did. Dorothy made a commitment to herself to continue to increase her charitable giving because she realized she had the means. John, who has been sitting on his unsigned will for four to five years, decided to talk to his partner, rewrite his will based on their conversation and sign it.

After our conversation, Liv wrote her memoir and presented copies as gifts to her family, and now her husband feels compelled to do the same. Phyllis is going to try to make amends with her brother because she doesn't want that fissure to be part of her legacy. Meredith is going to find a long-term volunteer commitment that could become the organization for her memorial donation. Henry and Derek are working to turn the lessons from their mentoring relationship into a training tool to create a legacy from what they learned together.

Distilled to their essence, these stories are about love, because life is a journey of the heart. By paying attention to our legacy, we are demonstrating our caring for one another, and we are expressing gratitude for this glorious gift of life. Now that I know more about KS's legacy, I understand that her life and her death embody this approach. She lived large and, at the same time, thought carefully about her afterlife. When her professional colleagues and the recipients of her scholarship speak and write about her, it is with admiration, gratitude and respect. Her family and friends talk about her the same way, and also with love and laughter.

As for me, writing this book has freed me from my narrow preoccupation with viewing KS's legacy as a memorial fund or tribute program. I understand that my grief was searching for a cosmic vehicle that would somehow embody my lost friend so we could be reunited. Now I accept that, while the public tributes are important, only the multi-faceted memories held in the minds of her beloved can do her full justice. KS loved to sing and that's how one friend remembers her. "Every time I hear a first soprano sing her notes with vigour and enthusiasm, I think of KS," the friend says. "She had a special way of conveying the musical message, be it in the church choir or at parties where the repertoire was more mundane. We had a good friendship, we laughed a lot together, but we also had serious discussions. And she's the only person to have ever swum around the island where we have our cottage. My husband followed her in a rowboat."

KS's sister emphasizes both KS's full-bore life and her meticulous preparation for death. "She was fully expecting to live forever and had fabulous plans for the future," she says. "But she left nothing undone. She poured herself into her boys while she was alive, and she was thinking of them and the rest of us by leaving her affairs in perfect order. And I just realized that it's because of her influence that I'm now trying to live a bit larger. At our choir, KS loved the spotlight and was very comfortable standing out. I was always content to be in the background. Now, at my advanced age, I'm taking her lead and coming out. I'm putting on a solo recital, complete with printed program, and inviting my family and friends to the performance. I guess this show honours my sister's legacy to me."

I can bring KS back in a flash. Here we are on a road trip in her Volvo—an amazing car for a university student, but her older brother had a dealership and wanted her to be safe. Our ritual on these trips was to recite Monty Python skits to one another, trying to outdo each other with cleverness. This time, one or the other of us scored big—maybe it was with the "Dead Parrot" skit—and we were in gales of laughter, tears streaming down our faces. KS had to pull the car to the side of the road until we calmed down. And when we got back on the road, we called a "time out" to pull ourselves together. Knowing her delightful and quirky sense of humour, I suppose an appropriate memorial for KS from my perspective would be a scholarship to a wacky comedy troupe. But that's just one of the memories I have of her, and there are countless more, each one highlighting yet another aspect of her multi-layered being. And as you have read, I'm only one of the many, many people who still feel her presence deeply.

KS's life is a lesson in accepting life's duality and acknowledging the double-pronged nature of legacy. If I were to follow her lead, I would strive to live as though I have all the time in the world to realize my dreams and make a contribution, while accepting that I may die at any moment. I would practise feeling profoundly alive in the moment at the same time that I am sensing the warm breath of death on my cheek. I would make thoughtful preparations for the end while maintaining a vise-like grip on life everlasting. Mainly, I would try to follow her example of living a life that makes a difference while leaving a legacy of love and laughter.

Acknowledgements

This book has been greatly enriched by the stories of over five dozen people. I am deeply grateful to them for entrusting me with the intimate details of their lives. To respect their confidences, I have changed their names and disguised identifying characteristics. Their candour gives us a unique window into challenging and sometimes painful situations, and I thank them profoundly for their generosity of spirit. I would also like to thank the reviewers, who gave me valuable feedback on an early draft of the book. They are Rita Bode, Peter Brimacombe, Leah Eustace, Jim Fletcher, Franklyn Griffiths, Andrea Intven, Hank Intven, Pam Katunar, Dustin Marnell, Marcia McClung and Marni Whitaker. The book has benefitted greatly from their knowledge and insights. Once again, my publisher and editor, Patrick Crean, has earned my undying gratitude for making the book the best it could be. And, as always, it's a dream to be supported by the excellence of the HarperCollins team. An eternal thank you goes to Hank, Lauren, Andrea, Diego and Zach, who make all things possible.

Notes

Background

1. Ed Koren, *The New Yorker*, November 27, 2017, p. 77.

Walking with Coffins

1. Julian Barnes, *Nothing to Be Frightened Of* (Toronto: Vintage Canada Edition, 2009), p. 65.
2. Ibid., p. 126.
3. See the website *deathcafe.com*.
4. Robert Matas, "An Artist in an Unlikely Residence," *The Globe and Mail*, May 28, 2005.
5. Jen St. Denis, "Remembering All the Souls at a Vancouver Graveyard," *Metro News*, October 28, 2016, http://www.metronews.ca/news/vancouver/2016/10/28/all-souls-at-mountain-view-offers-place-to-reflect.html.
6. See the website *https://nightforallsouls.com*.
7. Erika Hayasaki, *The Death Class: A True Story about Life* (New York: Simon & Schuster Paperbacks, 2014), p. 45.
8. Quoted in Barnes, *Nothing to Be Frightened Of*, p. 205.
9. Jody Porter, "Gord Downie's Secret Path Brings Hope to Chanie Wenjack's Family, 50 Years after Boy's Death," CBC News, October 18, 2016, http://www.cbc.ca/news/canada/thunder-bay/wenjack-family-response-secret-path-1.3808589.
10. See the website *www.downiewenjack.ca*.

Changing Our Lives

1. As described by Mrs. Cratchit, mother of Tiny Tim, in *A Christmas Carol* by Charles Dickens (London: Harper Press, 2010), p. 59.

2. Ibid., p. 99.

3. Ibid., p. 82.

4. Ibid., p. 39.

5. Ibid., p. 40.

6. Mari Ruti, *The Call of Character: Living a Life Worth Living* (New York: Columbia University Press, 2014), p. 9.

7. George F. MacDonald, *Ninstints: Haida World Heritage Site* (Vancouver: UBC Press, 1990), p.1.

8. From an information placard in The Bill Reid Rotunda, Museum of Anthropology, Vancouver, BC.

9. Bill Reid, "Curriculum Vitae 1," *Solitary Raven: The Essential Writings of Bill Reid*, Robert Bringhurst (ed.) (Vancouver: Douglas & McIntyre, 2009), p. 115.

10. Doris Shadbolt, "The Will to Be Haida," *Bill Reid and Beyond: Expanding on Modern Native Art*, Karen Duffek and Charlotte Townsend-Gault (eds.) (Toronto: Douglas & McIntyre, 2004), p. 35.

11. Miles Richardson, "On Its Own Terms," *Bill Reid and Beyond: Expanding on Modern Native Art*, Karen Duffek and Charlotte Townsend-Gault (eds.) (Toronto: Douglas & McIntyre, 2004), p. 22.

12. Brad Gooch, *Rumi's Secret: The Life of the Sufi Poet of Love* (New York: HarperCollins, 2017), p.123.

13. Ibid., p. 174.

14. Ibid., p. 124.

15. Ibid., p. 185.

16. *The Essential Rumi*, Translation by Coleman Barks, New Expanded Edition (New York: Harper One, 2004), p. xv.

17. Ibid., p. 41.

Living Our Legacies

1. For more on these athletes, see Melissa Renwick, "How the Surfing Sisterhood Helped Put Tofino on the Map," *The Globe and Mail,* March 7, 2018, https://www.theglobeandmail.com/news/british-columbia/surfing-sisterhood-of-tofino/article38231777/.

2. Kim Gray, "Surfer Girls Find Nirvana Catching Waves in Tofino," *Calgary Herald*, July 17, 2014, http://www.calgaryherald.com/travel/Surfer+-girls+find+nirvana+catching+waves+Tofino/10038462/story.html.

3. See the website *www.surfsister.com*.

4. See the website *www.queenofthepeak.com*.

5. Nora Martin, "Kindergarten Students Build Their Surfing Skills," *Ha-Shilth-Sa*, May 2, 2016, https://www.hashilthsa.com/news/2016-05-02/kindergarten-students-build-their-surfing-skills.

Leaving Ourselves in Others

1. Sarah Petrescu, "Diverse Crowd Pays Tribute to Homeless Man Peter Verin," *Times Colonist*, January 19, 2017, http://www.timescolonist.com/news/local/diverse-crowd-pays-tribute-to-homeless-man-peter-verin-1.8063201.

2. Sarah Petrescu, "Peter Verin, UVic's Reluctant Philosopher King, Dies at 71," *Times Colonist*, January 12, 2017, http://www.timescolonist.com/news/local/peter-verin-uvic-s-reluctant-philosopherking-dies-at-71-1.7101837.

3. Spotted in Victoria, November 19, 2014, "To the homeless man named Peter who is always around Quadra/Mckenzie area, shout out to you for being one of the most humble and Intelligent people I've ever talked to!" Facebook Post, https://www.facebook.com/spottedvictoria/posts/747862145251255, retrieved May 24, 2018.

4. Petrescu, "Diverse Crowd Pays Tribute to Homeless Man Peter Verin."

5. Greg Pratt, "Post-secondary Staple Peter Verin Dies at 71," *Nexus*, January 16, 2017, http://www.nexusnewspaper.com/2017/01/16/postsecondary-staple-peter-verin-dies-at-71/.

Who Tells Our Story

1. Dave Eggers, "Introduction," *The Autobiographer's Handbook*, Jennifer Traig (ed.) (New York: Holt Paperbacks, 2008), p. 8.

2. Mark Medley, "Memoirist Revealed Residential-School Abuse," *The Globe and Mail*, April 1, 2017, p. S18.

3. Justice Institute of British Columbia, *Working Together*, Annual Report 08 09, http://www-files.jibc.ca/main/pdf/JIBC-Annual-Report-08-09.pdf.

4. Bruce Feiler, "The Stories That Bind Us," *The New York Times*, March 15, 2013,http://www.nytimes.com/2013/03/17/fashion/the-family-stories-that-bind-us-this-life.html.

5. Robert Brooks, "The Stories of Our Families: How Much Do We Truly Know?" *Dr.RobertBrooks.com*, November 21, 2013, http://www.drrobertbrooks.com/the-stories-of-our-families-how-much-do-we-truly-know/.

6. See the website *storycorps.org*.

7. See www.canada.ca/en/services/culture/history-heritage/genealogy-family-history.html.

8. See their website, *www.editors.ca*.

9. One online source is *legacybox.com*.

10. Paul Alexander, *Rough Magic* (New York: Da Capo Press, 1999), p. 339.

11. Diane Middlebrook, *Her Husband: Ted Hughes and Sylvia Plath—A Marriage* (New York: Viking, 2003), p. 227.

12. Ibid., p. 235.

13. Alexander, *Rough Magic*, p. 252.

14. Middlebrook, *Her Husband: Ted Hughes and Sylvia Plath—A Marriage*, p. 232.

15. Ibid., p. 237.

16. Alexander, *Rough Magic*, p. 335.

17. Ibid., p. 353.

18. Sylvia Plath, *The Letters of Sylvia Plath: Volume 1: 1940–1956*, Peter K. Steinberg and Karen Kukil (eds.) (New York: HarperCollins, 2017).

19. Middlebrook, *Her Husband: Ted Hughes and Sylvia Plath—A Marriage*, p. xviii.

20. Rachel Corbett, *You Must Change Your Life: The Story of Rainer Maria Rilke and Auguste Rodin* (New York: W.W. Norton & Company, 2016), p. 109.

21. Ibid.

22. Carole Gerson, "Maud's Darkening Gables," *Literary Review of Canada*, July/August 2017, p. 26.

23. Brad Gooch, *Rumi's Secret: The Life of the Sufi Poet of Love* (New York: HarperCollins, 2017), p. 86.

24. Maria Tippett, *Emily Carr: A Biography* (Toronto: House of Anansi Press Inc., 1994), p. 280.

25. Ibid., p. 303.

26. Emily Carr, *Hundreds and Thousands: The Journals of Emily Carr* (Madeira Park, BC: Douglas & McIntyre, 2013), p. 298.

27. Tippett, *Emily Carr: A Biography*, p. 153.

28. Susan Crean (ed.), *Opposite Contraries: The Unknown Journals of Emily Carr and Other Writings* (Vancouver: Douglas and McIntyre, 2003), p. 2.

29. Carol Pearson, *Emily Carr As I Knew Her* (Victoria, BC: TouchWood Editions, 2016), p. 153.

30. Ibid., p. 12.

31. Tippett, *Emily Carr: A Biography*, p. 274.

32. Carr, *Hundreds and Thousands: The Journals of Emily Carr*, p. 4.

33. Ibid., p. 44.

34. Ibid., p. 399.

35. Ibid., p. 24.

36. Ibid., p. 39.

37. Ibid., p. 195.

38. See the website *deadsocial.org*.

39. Sprebas, December 2, 2012, *Terry Pratchett:* Choosing to Die—*Intro Speech*, YouTube video file, https://www.youtube.com/watch?v=B8wkeNDAGyM.

40. BBC News, "Sir Terry Pratchett, Renowned Fantasy Author, Dies Aged 66," *BBC.com*, March 12, 2015, http://www.bbc.com/news/entertainment-arts-31858156.

41. Louise Lewis, "The Fiduciary Role," STEP *Journal*, February 2018. STEP is the global professional association for practitioners who specialize in family inheritance and succession planning.

42. BBC News, "Terry Pratchett's Unpublished Works Crushed by Steamroller," *BBC.com*, August 30, 2017, http://www.bbc.com/news/uk-england-dorset-41093066.

43. Nick Bilton, "The Upside to Technology? It's Personal," *The New York Times*, March 30, 2016, https://www.nytimes.com/2016/03/31/fashion/social-media-technology.html.

44. CBC Radio, "When His Father Died, This Technologist Created a Chatbot, so His Kids Could Talk to Their Grandfather," *CBC.ca*, February 25, 2018, http://www.cbc.ca/radio/spark/when-his-father-died-this-technologist-created-a-chatbot-so-his-kids-could-talk-to-their-grandfather-1.4548924.

45. James Vlahos, Interview by Lulu Garcia-Navarro, "Creating a 'Dad-bot' to Talk with a Dead Father," NPR Northwest Public Broadcasting, July 23, 2017, https://www.npr.org/2017/07/23/538825555/creating-a-dadbot-to-talk-with-a-dead-father.

46. James Vlahos, "A Son's Race to Give His Dying Father Artificial Immor-tality," *Wired*, July 18, 2017, https://www.wired.com/story/a-sons-race-to-give-his-dying-father-artificial-immortality/.

47. Hayley Tsukayama, "How the Tupac 'Hologram' Works," *The Washington Post*, April 18, 2012, https://www.washingtonpost.com/business/technology/how-the-tupac-hologram-works/2012/04/18/gIQA1ZVyQT_story.html?utm_term=.11ec8cda40d6.

48. TMZ, "Tupac's Mom—Coachella Hologram was Frickin' AMAZING" *TMZ.com*, April 16, 2012, http://www.tmz.com/2012/04/16/tupac-mother-afeni-shakur-coachella-hologram/.

49. Cathy Scott, "Rapper Tupac Shakur's Digital Resurrection Gets Mixed Reviews," *Forbes.com*, April 18, 2012, https://www.forbes.com/sites/crime/2012/04/18/rapper-tupac-shakurs-digital-resurrection-gets-mixed-reviews/#72d6cd9d4c7e.

50. Rap-Up, "Tupac Shakur Inducted into Rock & Roll Hall of Fame," *Rap-Up.com*, April 8, 2017, http://www.rap-up.com/2017/04/08/tupac-shakur-inducted-into-rock-roll-hall-of-fame/.

51. Lama Nachman, Interview by Laura Lynch, *The Current*, CBC Radio, March 20, 2018, http://www.cbc.ca/radio/thecurrent/the-current-for-march-20-2018-1.4583785/meet-the-woman-who-saved-stephen-hawking-s-voice-and-then-gave-the-technology-away-to-those-in-need-1.4583922.

History Will Have Its Way with Us

1. University of Victoria, June 2, 2017, *Trutch Name to Be Removed from Residence*, Press Release, https://www.uvic.ca/home/about/campus-news/2017+trutch-residence-renaming+ring.

2. Cision, "*The Beaver*: Canada's History Magazine Releases Results of 'Worst Canadians' Survey," *Newswire.ca*, July 30, 2017, http://www.newswire.ca/news-releases/the-beaver-canadas-history-magazine-releases-re-sults-of-worst-canadians-survey-534026251.html.

3. YaleNews, "Yale Changes Calhoun College's Name to Honor Grace Murray Hopper," Yale University, February 11, 2017, http://news.yale .edu/2017/02/11/yale-change-calhoun-college-s-name-honor-grace-murray-hopper-0.

4. Paul Waldie, "Queen's Stripping Radler's Name from Business Wing," *The Globe and Mail*, September 21, 2005, https://www.theglobeandmail .com/news/national/queens-stripping-radlers-name-from-business-wing/ article1124051/.

5. Amisha Padnani, "How an Obits Project on Overlooked Women Was Born," *The New York Times*, March 8, 2018, https://nyti.ms/2D9Mq4H.

6. Raoul Peck, Interview by Tom Power, *q*, CBC Radio, February 24, 2017, http://www.cbc.ca/radio/q/friday-feb-24-2017-raoul-peck-reginald-edmund-and-more-1.3995507/raoul-peck-brings-james-baldwin-s-powerful-gaze-to-the-big-screen-1.3995526.

7. Darryl Pinckney, "Under the Spell of James Baldwin," *The New York Review of Books*, March 23, 2017, http://www.nybooks.com/articles/ 2017/03/23/under-spell-james-baldwin/.

8. Devoney Looser, *The Making of Jane Austen* (Baltimore, MD: Johns Hopkins University Press, 2017), p. 7.

9. Paula Byrne, *The Real Jane Austen: A Life in Small Things* (New York: HarperCollins, 2013), p. 6.

10. Looser, *The Making of Jane Austen*, p. 3.

11. Anthony Lane, "Last Laugh," *The New Yorker*, March 13, 2017, p. 77.

Instructions from the Grave

1. Jim Holt, "Two Brains Running," *The New York Times*, November 25, 2011, https://www.nytimes.com/2011/11/27/books/review/thinking-fast-and-slow-by-daniel-kahneman-book-review.html.

2. Jean Blacklock and Sarah Kruger, *The 50 Biggest Estate Planning Mistakes ... and How to Avoid Them* (Mississauga, ON: John Wiley & Sons Canada, 2011), p. 53.

3. Ian Mulgrew, "Hollow Tree Friendship Leads to Inheritance Squabble," *Vancouver Sun*, September 6, 2017, http://vancouversun.com/news/local-news/ian-mulgrew-hollow-tree-friendship-leads-to-inheritance-squabble.

4. Jon Hernandez, "What Eleanor Wanted: The Divisive 'Last Will' of a Hollow Tree Champion," *CBC.ca*, September 23, 2017, http://www.cbc.ca/ news/canada/british-columbia/what-eleanor-wanted-the-divisive-last-will-of-a-hollow-tree-champion-1.4298987.

5. See http://www.bankofcanada.ca/unclaimed-balances/.

6. Frances Backhouse, *Once They Were Hats: In Search of the Mighty Beaver* (Toronto: ECW Press, 2015), p. 76.

7. Ibid., p. 82.

8. Ibid., p. 83.

9. Lizzie Widdicombe, "Dem Bones," *The New Yorker*, April 10, 2017, p. 18.

10. Joshua Harmon wrote the play *Bad Jews* in 2011. The play has been performed around the world and has become one of the most produced plays in the United States. The quotations are from the Overlook Duckworth edition (New York, 2017).

11. Ibid., p. 26.

12. Marjo Johne, "Wealthy Canadians Cutting Children Out and Leaving Money to Charity," *The Globe and Mail*, retrieved March 25, 2017, https://www.theglobeandmail.com/globe-investor/personal-finance/wealthy-canadians-cut-children-out-charities-in/article15561416/.

The Dubious Honour

1. Max Brod, "Postscript to the First Edition (1925)," *The Trial*, Franz Kafka (New York: Schocken Books, 1992), p. 264.

2. Ibid., p. 265.

3. Ibid., p. 267.

4. Ibid.

5. Reiner Stach, *Is That Kafka?: 99 Finds*, translated by Kurt Beals (New York: New Directions Book, 2016), p. 132.

6. Reiner Stach, *Kafka: The Years of Insight*, translated by Shelley Frisch (Princeton, NJ: Princeton University Press, 2013), p. 477.

7. George Steiner, "Introduction," in *The Trial*, Franz Kafka (New York: Schocken Books, 1992), p. vii.

8. Paul Alexander, *Death and Disaster: The Rise of the Warhol Empire and the Race for Andy's Millions* (New York: Random House, Inc., 1994), p. 244.

9. Arthur C. Danto, *Andy Warhol* (New Haven: Yale University Press, 2009), p. 47.

10. Jane Wagner, *The Search for Signs of Intelligent Life in the Universe* (New York: Harper & Row, 1986), p. 29.

11. Victor Bockris, *The Life and Death of Andy Warhol* (New York: Bantam Books, 1989), p. 238.

12. Andy Warhol, *The Philosophy of Andy Warhol: From A to B and Back Again* (New York: Harcourt, Inc., 1975), p. 92.

13. Bockris, *The Life and Death of Andy Warhol*, p. 255.

14. Alexander, *Death and Disaster: The Rise of the Warhol Empire and the Race for Andy's Millions*, p. 155.

15. Ibid., p. 219.

16. See the website *warholfoundation.org*.

Giving Back

1. For details on Canadian charitable donations and volunteer activities, see Martin Turcotte, *Volunteering and Charitable Giving in Canada*, Statistics Canada 89-652-X 2016, http://www.stacan.gc.ca/pub/89-652-x/89-652-x2015001-eng.htm.

2. Terry Fox, Terry's Letter Requesting Support, *TerryFox.org*, http://www.terryfox.org/terrys-story/terrys-letter/.

3. The Terry Fox Foundation, "The Marathon of Hope," *TerryFox.org*, http://www.terryfox.org/terrys-story/marathon-of-hope/.

4. Tracy Gary, *Inspired Philanthropy* (San Francisco: Jossey-Bass, 2008), p. 10.

5. The survey was conducted on behalf of the Association of Fundraising Professionals (AFP) Foundation for Philanthropy–Canada by Ipsos. *What Canadian Donors Want,* http://www.afpnet.org/ResourceCenter/ArticleDetail.cfm?ItemNumber=36796.

6. See the website *www.imaginecanada.ca*.

7. See the website *www.canadahelps.org*.

8. To download electronic versions of the worksheets and exercises, go to www.inspiredlegacies.org.

9. Peter Singer, *The Most Good You Can Do* (New Haven: Yale University Press, 2015), p. 26.

10. Ibid., p. 16.

11. The Against Malaria Foundation provides funding for the distribution of insecticide-treated nets in developing countries, and the Schistosomiasis Control Initiative supports government-run deworming programs in low-income countries. See https://www.givewell.org/charities/top-charities.

12. Malcolm Gladwell, interview by Tyler Cowen, *Conversations*, March 15, 2017, https://medium.com/conversations-with-tyler/malcolm-gladwell-podcast-outliers-tyler-cowen-3abdf99068ee. For a response to Gladwell's general opposition to funding wealthy universities, see Mike Scutari, "The Sultan of Brunei? Really? Unpacking Malcolm Gladwell's Latest Salvo Against Stanford," *Inside Philanthropy*, https://www.insidephilanthropy .com/home/2017/3/7/the-spokesman-for-effective-altruism-strikes-again-on-gladwells-slightly-misguided-attack-on-stanford.

13. See the website *communityfoundations.ca*.

14. See the website *www.charityintelligence.ca*. Another source of information is *www.moneysense.ca*, which provides ratings of the 100 largest charities using grade ratings for categories they label "charity efficiency" and "fundraising efficiency."

15. The authoritative source of information on charities is the Canada Revenue Agency website. You can search by charity name and/or registration number to obtain detailed information. See http://www.cra-arc.gc.ca/ ebci/haip/srch/advancedsearch-eng.action.

16. Jean Blacklock and Sarah Kruger, *The 50 Biggest Estate Planning Mistakes . . . and How to Avoid Them* (Mississauga, ON: John Wiley & Sons Canada, 2011), p. 155.

17. CanadaHelps, "Donate Securities and Mutual Funds through CanadaHelps," CanadaHelps.org, https://www.canadahelps.org/en/why-canadahelps/ ways-to-give/benefits-of-donating-securities/.

18. KCI, "The Recognition Issue," *Philanthropic Trends Quarterly*, 2012: Issue 4, http://kciphilanthropy.com/download_trends/KCI%20Trends%20 English_Q4%202012.pdf.

19. Michèle Benoit, *The Personal Philanthropy Project*, March 2017, p. 6.

20. See the website *www.imaginecanada.ca*.

21. Gary, *Inspired Philanthropy*, p. 241.

22. The Giving Pledge, "History of the Pledge," *GivingPledge.org*, https:// givingpledge.org/About.aspx.

23. Richard I. Kirkland Jr. and Carrie Gottlieb, "Should You Leave It All to the Children?" *Fortune*, September 29, 1986, http://archive.fortune.com/ magazines/fortune/fortune_archive/1986/09/29/68098/index.htm. Buffett modified his thinking somewhat over the years and has made large donations to his children's foundations to reward them for the way they've been managing their philanthropy.

24. The Giving Pledge, "A Commitment to Philanthropy," *GivingPledge.org*, https://givingpledge.org/Pledger.aspx?id=172.

25. Rob Carrick, "How Helping Your Adult Kids Financially Became the New Normal," *The Globe and Mail*, July 27, 2017, https://www.theglobeandmail.com/globe-investor/personal-finance/genymoney/how-helping-your-adult-kids-financially-became-the-new-normal/article35816506/.

26. Marjo Johne, "Wealthy Canadians Cutting Children Out and Leaving Money to Charity," *The Globe and Mail*, accessed March 25, 2017, https://www.theglobeandmail.com/globe-investor/personal-finance/wealthy-canadians-cut-children-out-charities-in/article15561416/.

27. See the website *www.socialventurepartners.org*.

28. See the website *www.cleanstartbc.ca*.

29. See the website *www.toniic.com*. UBC's Sauder School and SFU both have significant programs in this area. See http://www.sauder.ubc.ca/Faculty/Research_Centres/Centre_for_Social_Innovation_and_Impact_Investing and http://www.radiussfu.com/.

30. See the website *chimp.net*.

31. A comparison to setting up your own private foundation can be found at http://www.canadagives.ca/donor-advised-funds/your-foundation-choices/. A comparison to using a community foundation can be found at http://www.canadagives.ca/donor-advised-funds/comparison-of-community-foundations/.

Leaving a Piece of Ourselves

1. A 2017 Age Wave/Merrill Lynch study posed the question "Which of the following are very important to pass on to your children or heirs?" Here are the percentage responses in each category: values and life lessons 62%, instructions and wishes to be fulfilled 53%, personal possessions of emotional value 43%, financial assets or real estate 32%. Age Wave/Merrill Lynch, "Finances in Retirement: New Challenges, New Solutions," 2017, https://www.ml.com/articles/age-wave-survey.html.

2. Daniel Gottlieb, *Letters to Sam: A Grandfather's Lessons on Love, Loss, and the Gifts of Life* (New York: Sterling Publishing Co., 2006), p. 14.

3. Ibid., p. 15.

4. See http://dignityincare.ca/en/toolkit.html.

5. Tracy Hanes, "Thinking of Her Son's Future, Above All," *Toronto Star*, October 15, 2010, p. L3.

6. SecretValet, July 15, 2014, *Video Message delivered in the future by SecretValet using an electronic time capsule*, YouTube video file, https://www.youtube.com/watch?v=JsCywQwspPQ.

7. Paul Sullivan, "Digital Messages for Loved Ones from Beyond the Grave," *The New York Times*, October 23, 2015, https://www.nytimes.com/2015/10/24/your-money/digital-messages-for-loved-ones-from-beyond-the-grave.html.

8. Candy Schulman, "My Motherless Mother," *The New York Times*, January 13, 2016, https://opinionator.blogs.nytimes.com/2016/01/13/my-motherless-mother/.

9. See the website *www.wpshc.com*.

10. Margareta Magnusson, *The Gentle Art of Swedish Death Cleaning* (New York: Scribner, 2018), p. 4.

11. Ibid., p. 104.

12. See the website *www.cantransplant.ca*.

13. See the website *concussionfoundation.org*.

14. Dylan Matthews, "Why I Gave My Kidney to a Stranger—And Why You Should Consider Doing It Too," *Vox*, April 11, 2017, https://www.vox.com/science-and-health/2017/4/11/12716978/kidney-donation-dylan-matthews.

15. germanrlopez, March 6, 2018, "Have to credit @dylanmatt for inspiring me to do this," Tweet, https://twitter.com/germanrlopez/status/971129480084324352?lang=en. For information about organ donation in Canada, visit the website of the Kidney Foundation of Canada, https://www.kidney.ca. The website includes links to provincial organ donor registries.

16. NYTDirect.com, "An estimated one in five adults in the United States have at least one tattoo," Morning Briefing *The New York Times*, email received March 13, 2018.

17. Charles Hamm, Interview by Shad, *q*, CBC Radio, October 15, 2015, http://www.cbc.ca/radio/q/schedule-for-wednesday-october-7-1.3260084/tattoo-preservationist-makes-case-for-saving-skin-art-1.3260099.

18. Reiss Smith, "What is cryogenics and how does freezing bodies work?" *Express*, November 18, 2016, https://www.express.co.uk/news/science/733717/What-is-cryogenics-how-does-freezing-dead-body-work.